Memory Puzzles
to Keep You Sharp

Test Your Recall with 80 Photo Games

LUKE SHARPE

PUZZLE
WRIGHT
PRESS
New York

PUZZLE
WRIGHT
PRESS

New York

An Imprint of Sterling Publishing Co., Inc.
1166 Avenue of the Americas
New York, NY 10036

ISBN 978-1-4549-2669-6

Distributed in Canada by Sterling Publishing Co., Inc.
C/o Canadian Manda Group, 664 Annette Street
Toronto, Ontario M6S 2C8, Canada
Distributed in the United Kingdom by GMC Distribution Services
Castle Place, 166 High Street, Lewes, East Sussex BN7 1XU, England
Distributed in Australia by NewSouth Books
45 Beach Street, Coogee, NSW 2034, Australia

For information about custom editions, special sales, and premium and
corporate purchases, please contact Sterling Special Sales at 800-805-5489 or
specialsales@sterlingpublishing.com.

Manufactured in China

2 4 6 8 10 9 7 5 3 1

sterlingpublishing.com
www.puzzlewright.com

Cover design by David Ter-Avanesyan based on an original design by Elizabeth Mihaltse Lindy
Egyptian papyrus by cobalt88/Shutterstock.com
Cat (cover and title page) by Rasulov/Shutterstock.com

Contents

Introduction

There's an old magic trick that's easy to perform and surprisingly effective. Begin by showing two cards: The 2 of hearts and the 3 of spades. After having your subject insert those cards separately into the deck, grip the deck tightly along its edge and say the magic word. Then rap the deck on the table and squeeze the top and bottom cards together while forcing the rest from between them. With practice, it will appear that you have pulled both of the original cards from the center of the deck.

How does it work? Before you showed the trick, you placed two *different* cards on the top and bottom of the deck: the 2 of spades and the 3 of hearts. In the time between seeing the first two cards and the different last two, the subject has likely forgotten which was which. Magicians know they can count on their audience's poor memory.

In this book, you'll get to find out just how good your memory is (and how much it improves by the end). On each right-hand page, there is a picture to study and an icon indicating the time limit, from three to six minutes. Photos that are oriented vertically and photos oriented horizontally are separated into their own sections, so you don't have to keep rotating the book as you go through it; within each section, the difficulty increases as you continue, as does the time limit. After examining the picture for the full amount of time, turn the page over; on the opposite side is a set of questions about the picture, ranging from easy to difficult. Some of the questions will ask about obvious features of the picture, and some will ask about small details.

For example, take a look at the picture at right. This photo isn't very detailed, so take just a minute or so to study it, if you'd like to try answering the sample questions on the next page.

Easy questions I might ask about that picture are "Is the man wearing a bow tie or a long necktie?" and "True or false: The man's ears are visible." A medium-difficulty question might be "What color Post-it appears on the man's head but not his shirt?" Finally, a hard question might be "How many Post-its are on the man's sleeves?" Easy questions are worth 1 point, medium questions are worth 3 points, and hard questions are worth 5 points. Some questions have bonus points available; for instance, the third question above might have asked, "What color Post-it appears on the man's head but not his shirt? And, for a bonus point, are all the Post-its of that color the same size?" Even if you don't answer the main question correctly, you can still earn the bonus points, unless otherwise specified in the question.

You can always check your answers by going back to look at the picture again, but you may find it easier to simply consult the back of the book. (The correct answers to the above questions are, respectively: a long necktie; false; pink, and no, the pink Post-its are not all the same size; and one.)

If you would like an extra challenge, you can increase the difficulty in one of two ways (earning extra points accordingly). You may reduce the time you study the picture; for each minute by which you reduce the time limit, you earn an extra 3 points, but to collect each minute's points you must answer at least one question correctly. So, for instance, if you study a picture with a 6-minute time limit for 3 minutes, but then answer only two questions correctly, you only earn 6 bonus points, not 9. Alternatively, you may study the picture for the full amount of time . . . and then step away from the book for a while before answering the questions. For each minute you wait between studying the photo and answering the questions, you earn 3 bonus points (but, as before, you must get at least one correct answer per minute to collect the extra points).

For *less* of a challenge, you may increase the time limit, subtracting 3 points from your overall score for each minute you add.

Try a few of these every day, and your memory may begin to improve . . . like magic.

—Luke Sharpe

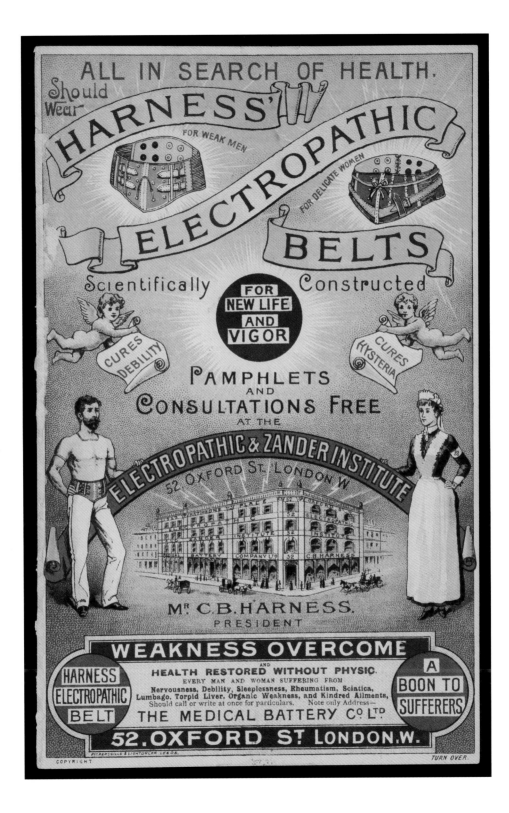

Easy questions (1 point):

1) Both a men's and a women's version of the belt are shown. What color is each?
   a) red for men, blue for women
   b) blue for men, red for women

2) Is the woman on the right wearing anything on her head?

3) What does the man on the left wear above his electropathic belt?
   a) a long-sleeved shirt
   b) a short-sleeved shirt
   c) nothing

4) Do the cherubs have halos?

Medium questions (3 points):

5) What is the name of the institute promoting the Electropathic Belts?

6) According to the illustration of the Institute, how many stories are above the street level?

7) Which word does NOT appear somewhere in the large dark circle near the ad's center?
   a) vigor
   b) life
   c) proven

8) What number on Oxford Street is home to the Institute?

9) How many black dots are visible inside each of the belts?

10) What two items are listed as "free" at the Institute?
    a) Pamphlets and Consultations
    b) Pamphlets and Demonstrations
    c) Fittings and Consultations
    d) Fittings and Demonstrations

Hard questions (5 points):

11) What is the name of the company promoting this ad, listed near the bottom?

12) What two items are cured, according to scrolls held by the two cherubs?

13) What is the name of the Institute's president, shown just beneath the building?
    a) Mr. C.W. Harness
    b) Mr. C.B. Harness
    c) Dr. C.W. Harness
    d) Dr. C.B. Harness

14) Complete this sentence from the box at the bottom of the ad: Health restored without ____.

Your score: _____
Maximum base score: 42
Answers, page 167

Easy questions (1 point):

1) True or false: The clock on the wall has a second hand.

2) Of the two girls dancing, one's hand is being held by the other. Whose hand is being held?
   a) the girl on the left
   b) the girl on the right

3) Are any of the girls' bare elbows visible in the scene?

4) For the dancing girl whose back is facing us, which apron string crosses over the other one—the string over her left shoulder, or the string over her right?

5) Does the T-square have a hole near its long end?

6) On the right side of the picture, a hand can be seen. Is it a right or a left hand?

Medium questions (3 points):

7) Which most closely describes what's on top of the display case?
   a) a stuffed pelican and a stuffed turtle
   b) a stuffed pelican and a globe
   c) a stuffed pelican and a stuffed alligator
   d) a model ship and a stuffed alligator

8) What is the seated girl in the center of the picture covering?

9) Which best describes the floor of the classroom?
   a) wooden planks
   b) solid color
   c) patterned carpet

10) What digit appears after "PH" at the top of the display case?

11) How is the hair of the girl in profile at the far left of the scene arranged?
   a) it is loose
   b) it is held back by a hairband and is in a bun
   c) it is in a ponytail

Hard questions (5 points):

12) How many buttons are visible on the front of the girl pretending to play the violin?
   a) approximately 8
   b) approximately 14
   c) approximately 20

13) In the space just under the right arm of the girl pretending to play the violin, what can we see a pair of?

Your score: _____
Maximum base score: 31
Answers, page 167

Easy questions (1 point):

1) True or false: None of the people in the scene are wearing glasses.

2) There is a bottle of ketchup on the cart near the door. Is it standing on its lid, or is the lid on the top?

3) Do any of the people in the scene have facial hair?

4) Does the decoration in the foreground center near the ceiling include a cross shape?

Medium questions (3 points):

5) What number appears backward on the front door?

6) How many people are in the scene?

7) Is the plant holder at the right brown, silver, or gold?

8) Which best describes the bistro's floor?
   a) wooden zigzags
   b) patterned carpet
   c) square ceramic tiles

9) When was the bistro established?

10) What is the main color of the stained-glass flowers in the scene?

11) Which best describes the design of the front window?
   a) concentric circles (like a target) divided by two straight vertical lines
   b) concentric circles divided by two straight horizontal lines
   c) non-concentric circles divided by two straight vertical lines
   d) non-concentric circles divided by two straight horizontal lines

12) How many bent-wood chairs can be seen at the left?

Hard questions (5 points):

13) Two sets of salt-and-pepper shakers can be seen on empty tables. Where are they?
   a) on the far right and far left of the picture
   b) on the far right and the table near the front window
   c) on the far left and the table near the front window

14) What appears in the upper right corner of the bistro, near the ceiling by the front window?

15) What is the main color of the beer label on the bottle in front of the man in the black hoodie? For 3 extra points, what shape is it?

Your score: _____
Maximum base score: 46
Answers, page 167

Easy questions (1 point):

1) True or false: The scout's shirt has a breast pocket.

2) What is at the top ends of the flag sticks the scout is holding against his body?
   a) tapering points
   b) round balls
   c) the flat ends of the dowels

3) Does the strap that runs across the scout's chest go over or under his bandanna?

Medium questions (3 points):

4) Is the scout wearing a belt through his belt loops?
   a) yes
   b) no
   c) we can't tell

5) One badge depicts a series of faces and a patriotic emblem. How many faces are shown?

6) What holds the group of flag sticks together?
   a) the boy's closed fist
   b) twine
   c) a rubber band

7) The scout is wearing a red bandanna with a thin line of a second color. What color is that line?

8) What symbol appears on the middle badge in the second row?

9) How many of the round badges have a red ring around them?
   a) none
   b) approximately four
   c) approximately eight

10) The point where the scout's bandanna gathers is held by a slide that has something extending from either side. What is that?
    a) arrows
    b) wings
    c) stars

Hard questions (5 points):

11) The long end of an adjustable strap hangs down from the scout's waist. Compared to his wristwatch in the photo, is the strap's end higher, lower, or at the same height?

12) Hanging near the bottom of the photo is the scout's cap, which is a khaki color. What color is the button at the top of the cap?
    a) khaki
    b) white
    c) blue

13) How many of the scout's fingernails are visible in the scene?

Your score: _____
Maximum base score: 39
Answers, page 167

Easy questions (1 point):

1) True or false: The yellow bow above the year is drawn symmetrically.

2) Is the pointy side of the ship on the left or the right?

3) Are all the stars in the outer border, between the leaves, oriented in the same direction?

Medium questions (3 points):

4) What is the year shown?

5) How many white supports extend from the ship to the ground?
   a) 6
   b) 8
   c) 10

6) What best describes the rays of the sun?
   a) just gold triangles
   b) just gray lines
   c) alternating gold triangles and gray lines

7) How many stars appear in the outer border, between the leaves?

8) What color are the long banners waving at the top of the ship's masts?

9) What belongs in the blank? ___ OF THE STATE OF NEW HAMPSHIRE
   a) GREAT SEAL
   b) SEAL
   c) SHIELD
   d) CREST

Hard questions (5 points):

10) How many white stripes appear on the U.S. flag on the ship?

11) What best describes the border's concentric circles, near the words?
    a) there is one inside the words and one outside them
    b) there are two inside the words and two outside them
    c) there is one inside the words and two outside them
    d) there are two inside the words and one outside them

12) What is notable about the space between the words NEW and HAMPSHIRE?

Your score: _____
Maximum base score: 36
Answers, page 167

Easy questions (1 point):

1) There is a heart-shaped lollipop in the scene. Does it rest against the right or left side of the compartment it's in?

2) True or false: There are nails visible in the wood frame.

3) Are there more open containers or closed containers visible in the display?

4) Can any candy be seen in the small sliver of a compartment at the bottom center of the photograph?

Medium questions (3 points):

5) Does the wood paneling in the back of the shelves run vertically, horizontally, or diagonally?

6) How many small jars are lined up next to each other in the third compartment on the top?

7) Which combination of colors does not appear on any of the candy canes?
a) red and white stripes
b) green and white stripes
c) green and yellow stripes
d) red, white, and green stripes

8) How many compartments in the display can be seen in their entirety?

Hard questions (5 points):

9) There is a jar with three round, swirly lollipops in it. What color is visible inside the jar itself?

10) What is inside the tallest jar with a knobbed lid?

11) Three of the compartments at the top have two boards as their back wall. One compartment has a different number. How many boards make up that compartment's back wall?

12) At the upper right corner is a jar with four spherical lollipops. Two of the four are the same color. What color are they?

Your score: _____
Maximum base score: 36
Answers, page 167

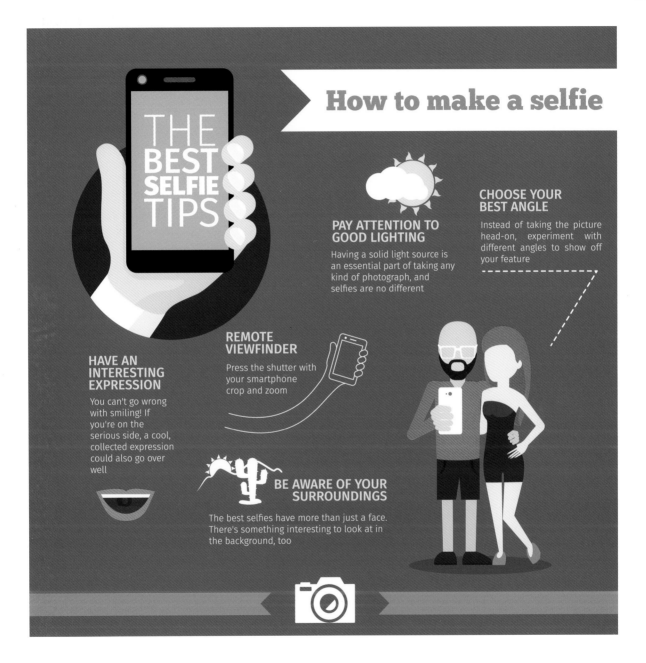

THE BEST SELFIE TIPS

How to make a selfie

PAY ATTENTION TO GOOD LIGHTING

Having a solid light source is an essential part of taking any kind of photograph, and selfies are no different

CHOOSE YOUR BEST ANGLE

Instead of taking the picture head-on, experiment with different angles to show off your feature

HAVE AN INTERESTING EXPRESSION

You can't go wrong with smiling! If you're on the serious side, a cool, collected expression could also go over well

REMOTE VIEWFINDER

Press the shutter with your smartphone crop and zoom

BE AWARE OF YOUR SURROUNDINGS

The best selfies have more than just a face. There's something interesting to look at in the background, too

Easy questions (1 point):

1) Is the large hand at the top a left or a right hand?

2) True or false: The woman has no features on her face.

3) Are there any exclamation points in the picture?

4) For the smiling mouth at the lower left, can you see teeth on the top and bottom, or just on the top?

Medium questions (3 points):

5) What color is the man's shirt?

6) How many sun rays can be seen on the yellow sun, including the ray that's partially obscured?
a) 6
b) 8
c) 10

7) Is the woman wearing earrings, a necklace, or neither?

8) What color is the ribbon at the bottom?

9) The thumbs of the man and woman don't show, but the rest of their fingers do, on the hands you can see. How many fingers can be seen on each hand?

10) What does it say in the white ribbon at the top?
a) How to take a selfie
b) How to make a selfie
c) How to take the best selfies

11) How many arms are coming off the main section of the cactus?

Hard questions (5 points):

12) How many times, combined, do the words "selfie" or "selfies" appear in the picture?
a) 2
b) 4
c) 6
d) 8

13) Only one of the tip headings, which is in the center of the picture, has no verb. What is that heading?

Your score: _____
Maximum base score: 35
Answers, page 167

Easy questions (1 point):

1) True or false: No one in the scene is wearing glasses.

2) In which direction is the person with the pink backpack at the right of the picture facing, right or left?

3) Does the red paint on the pavilion show any wear?

4) Which is higher, the top of the tree at the far right or the tips of the upward-curving corners of the pavilion's roof?

5) Utility wires can be seen to the right of the pavilion. Can they be seen on the left?

Medium questions (3 points):

6) How many tall, rectangular window panels are there along the front side of the pavilion on the second floor?
   a) 4
   b) 6
   c) 8

7) What kind of creature is depicted in the sculpture on the peak of the roof at the right?

8) What is the covered bridge resting on?
   a) collections of large stones
   b) wooden pillars
   c) sculptures of animal figures

9) What two colors are the hair of the woman at the left in the pink jacket?

10) How many poles supporting the roof of the covered bridge can be seen on the side of the bridge closest to the camera?

Hard questions (5 points):

11) The most decorative sections of the fencing on the second floor of the pavilion are made of T and L shapes. What best describes the T's?
   a) they appear only right side up
   b) they appear only upside down
   c) they appear right side up and upside down
   d) they appear in all four orientations

12) There is a window on a building in the background at the right with four narrow vertical panels (each made of four squares). Counting from the left, which of its four panels is open?

Your score: _____
Maximum base score: 30
Answers, page 167

HOMENAGEM AO CINEMA

S. TOMÉ E PRÍNCIPE

Easy questions (1 point):

1) True or false: One of the movie titles ends with an exclamation point.

2) Which stamp is farther left, the one for "King Kong" or the one for "Stagecoach"?

3) Do the perforations go all the way from top to bottom and all the way from left to right across the sheet?

Medium questions (3 points):

4) How many cancellation marks does the sheet of stamps contain?

5) Which one of these movies is not represented by one of the stamps?
   a) "Gone With the Wind"
   b) "Wee Willie Winkie"
   c) "The Wizard of Oz"
   d) "Oregon Trail"

6) What well-known landmark is depicted on the stamp in the lower left corner?

7) The edges of many of the movie poster images were badly cropped in order to fit the available space on the stamps. What word from one of the movie titles is cropped so extensively that little more than its top half appears?

8) What is the value of each of the stamps, as shown consistently across all nine stamps?
   a) Db 1000
   b) Dd 1000
   c) Db 10000
   d) Dd 10000

9) One of the images shows a man at the helm of a ship. How many of his hands are shown?

10) What kind of animal appears most often on the stamps?

11) Who gets top billing in "The Oklahoma Kid"?

12) In the margins of the sheet are repeated designs meant to evoke strips of film. In each design, how many frames (that is, large black boxes) appear?

Hard questions (5 points):

13) Only one of the movie titles is rendered horizontally without being at all skewed, at an angle, or with its letters at varied heights or on a curve. Which title is that?

14) In small print beneath each image is a date, followed by a slash mark and a capital letter. What are the date and capital letter?

15) At the bottom of the sheet of stamps is the name of the island nation that issued them. How many accented letters are in this name?

Your score: _____
Maximum base score: 45
Answers, page 167

24

Easy questions (1 point):

1) True or false: There are no face cards (jacks, queens, and kings).

2) Which card appears on a higher level, the 10 of hearts or the 10 of diamonds?

3) Are there any aces?

Medium questions (3 points):

4) How many levels are in this house of cards? For a bonus point, how many horizontal "floor" levels are there?

5) What two colors are on the backs of the cards?

6) There is only one 9. What is its suit?

7) Where do the numbers appear on each card?
   a) at the upper left and lower right
   b) at the upper right and lower left
   c) in all four corners

8) The two cards at the top are the same suit. What suit?

9) Looking at the two 2's, how many of the larger pips (not the small ones in the corners) are visible on these two cards?
   a) both are visible on each card
   b) one is visible on each card
   c) both are visible on one card, and one is visible on the other

Hard questions (5 points):

10) There are no cards of any suit for one of the values from 2 through 10. Which is the missing number?

11) Each suit is represented here the same number of times. How many cards appear in each suit?

12) What best describes the shape of the O's in the number 10's?
    a) round
    b) oval
    c) square with rounded corners
    d) rectangular with rounded corners

13) Counting from the top, which level has the lowest percentage of red cards?

14) How many of the card values appear four times—that is, how many fours of a kind are there?

Your score: _____
Maximum base score: 47
Answers, page 168

TO·THE·GLORY·OF·GOD   ·AND·IN·LOVING·MEMORY·OF·   ·GRACE·DORGAN·PORTER·

Easy questions (1 point):

1) One angel at the top is wearing yellow and the other is wearing green. Which color is on the left?

2) True or false: The man in the middle panel is wearing sandals.

3) Is there a child in the scene?

4) Which are higher, the hands of the man kneeling at the left or the hands of the man kneeling at the right?

Medium questions (3 points):

5) How many people in the scene have facial hair?

6) What is the name of the person in whose memory the window is dedicated?
   a) Grace Porter Dorgan
   b) Grace Dorgan Porter
   c) Porter Grace Dorgan

7) What two colors (besides black) appear on the container into which liquid is being poured?

8) Which of these best describes the columned structure in the background?
   a) It extends through all three main panels and has nothing hanging from it
   b) It extends through two of the main panels and has nothing hanging from it
   c) It extends through all three main panels and is partially hidden by a piece of fabric in one panel and a garland of flowers in another
   d) It extends through two of the main panels and is partially hidden by a piece of fabric in one panel and a garland of flowers in another

9) How many people in the scene are wearing fabric draped on their heads?

10) What color are the wings of the angels at the top of the window?

Hard questions (5 points):

11) The bottom of the window includes a series of blue and red shapes in a row. How many are red?

12) What objects are scattered on the floor in the middle panel?

13) Starting with the line that crosses the containers on the floor in each of the three main panels and moving upward to the point of each panel's arch, how many horizontal black lines cross the entirety of each panel?

Your score: _____
Maximum base score: 37
Answers, page 168

Easy questions (1 point):

1) Are any of the words in capital letters?

2) True or false: The word "lightbulb" appears prominently in the image.

3) Which style of type is used for the letters, sans serif (unadorned letters made mostly of straight lines and curves, like the type used in these questions) or serif (letters with small decorative projections at the ends of the lines)?

4) Are any of the words so small that they are inside the letters of other words?

5) Which style of the letter "g" is used: one with an "open tail" or one with an enclosed "loop tail"?

Medium questions (3 points):

6) What is the largest word in the image? For 2 bonus points, how else does it differ from all the other words?

7) In which color is the large word "brilliant" rendered?
   a) red
   b) orange
   c) yellow
   d) gray

8) Put these large yellow words in order from top to bottom: business, process, product

9) There is only one large gray word long enough to span the width of the lightbulb's "base." What word is that?
   a) engineering
   b) communication
   c) information
   d) technology
   e) revolution

Hard questions (5 points):

10) Which two of these appear among the words in the word cloud? Give yourself 5 points for each one.
    a) punctuation marks
    b) Arabic numbers (numerical symbols like 1, 2, 3)
    c) proper nouns (words ordinarily capitalized)
    d) hyphenated words (like "twenty-one")
    e) contractions (combined and shortened words like "can't")
    f) initialisms (initials that are rendered without periods)

11) What word appears in small letters at the very bottom of the word cloud?

12) Some of the largest words are centered left-to-right in the image. Which one of these is not one of those large, centered words?
    a) goal
    b) idea
    c) users
    d) business
    e) creativity

Your score: _____
Maximum base score: 39
Answers, page 168

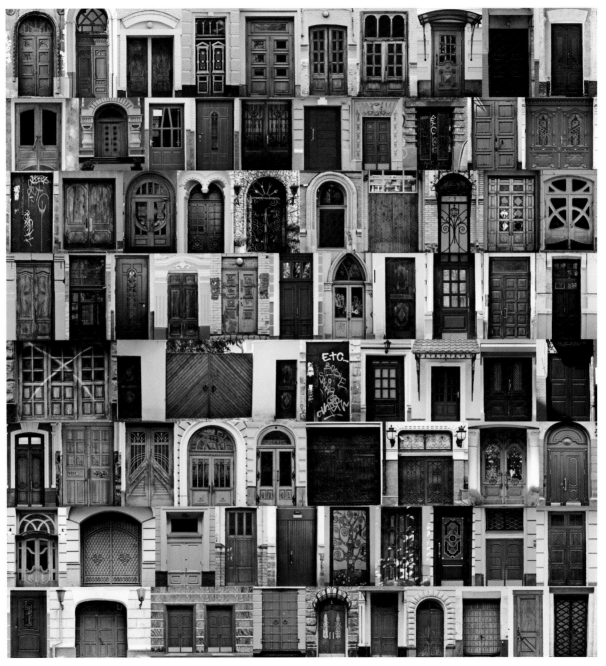

Easy questions (1 point):

1) There is a red door in the rightmost column. Is it a single door or a double door?

2) True or false: There is no greenery in the picture.

3) Which is farther to the right, the blue door with the double-arched yellow frame, or the wooden door with the frame that's yellow on the top and orange on the bottom?

Medium questions (3 points):

4) How many rows of doors appear in the picture?

5) One door has a fanciful painting. What does it depict?
a) a head with snakes for hair
b) swirling smoke
c) a tree with curved branches

6) What three-letter abbreviation appears spray-painted on multiple doors with graffiti on them? For an extra 3 points, how many times does it appear?

7) There is one triple door shown, with three identical panels side-by-side. What is its main material?
a) dark metal
b) brown wood
c) a material painted black

Hard questions (5 points):

8) How many doorframes clearly come to a point at the top?
a) 1
b) 4
c) 7

9) One door has a dappled sun effect covering most of the door. Counting from the bottom, which row is it in?

10) There is a purple door in the bottom right quadrant. How many light fixtures are next to it?
a) 0
b) 1
c) 2

Your score: _____
Maximum base score: 33
Answers, page 168

BODY WATER
— Health & Medical —
INFOGRAPHICS

HOW MUCH DO YOU REALLY NEED?

| BODY WEIGHT /2 (lbs) | 1 = 8 OUNCES | WATER NEEDED PER DAY |

BODY 70% WATER

DRINK MORE WATER

 BRAIN 75% WATER

 LUNGS 90% WATER

 BONES 24% WATER

 HELPS CONVERT FOOD INTO ENERGY

 BLOOD 85% WATER

 SKIN 80% WATER

 MUSCLE 75% WATER

 HELPS BODY ABSORB NUTRIENTS

Easy questions (1 point):

1) Who is wearing a light blue top, the man or the woman?

2) Does the "bones" information appear on the left side or the right side of the picture?

3) Do the percent signs have two free-floating circles, or is the top circle connected to the slash?

Medium questions (3 points):

4) What color are the eyes of the people who are drinking?

5) What is the water droplet saying?
   a) drink more water
   b) you need water
   c) drink lots of water

6) The section in the middle right shows text in three colored balloons. What is the order of the colors, from left to right?
   a) green, blue, black
   b) green, black, blue
   c) blue, black, green
   d) blue, green, black
   e) black, green, blue
   f) black, blue, green

7) Which is shown to have the highest percentage of water?
   a) blood
   b) brain
   c) lungs
   d) muscle
   e) skin

8) What color are the dotted lines that separate the sections on the right?

9) What are the positions of the arms on the water droplet?
   a) one up, one down
   b) both up (making muscles)
   c) the droplet doesn't have arms, only legs

Hard questions (5 points):

10) How many small bumps appear on each side of the large water bottle?

11) Which one of the three lines of text at the top appears in upper and lowercase?
   a) Body Water
   b) Health & Medical
   c) Infographics

12) How many fingers are shown on each visible hand of the man and woman?

Your score: _____
Maximum base score: 36
Answers, page 168

Easy questions (1 point):

1) Which is higher, the bill from the Cook Islands or the bill with the waving man?

2) Is there a bill from Nigeria?

3) Is the standing man near the top with his arms crossed looking to our right or our left?

Medium questions (3 points):

4) How many U.S. bills can be seen in whole or in part? For an extra point apiece, what are their denominations?

5) From what country is the purple bill with the rhinoceros?
   a) Brazil
   b) Suriname
   c) Tanzania

6) What denomination is the bill near the center with a bird on it?
   a) 1
   b) 2
   c) 5
   d) 10

7) How many giraffes can be seen on the South Sudanese pound?
   a) 6
   b) 8
   c) 10

Hard questions (5 points):

8) A piece of a reddish bill can be seen at the right, marked K50. What currency does the bill indicate the K stands for?
   a) krone
   b) kwacha
   c) kyat

9) What is the denomination of the bill at the far right that is immediately to the right of the 5-euro bill?

10) Which of these denominations can be seen on the centrally placed lire bill from Italy, which shows a portrait of a woman?
   a) the number 1000
   b) the word MILLE
   c) both the number 1000 and the word MILLE

Your score: _____
Maximum base score: 33
Answers, page 168

Easy questions (1 point):

1) Is there a pineapple in the picture?

2) There are two groups of blueberries, a large group of small ones and a small group of large ones. Which group appears immediately below the two eggplants?

3) Do the carrots still have their greenery attached?

4) There are two bunches of diagonally placed grapes near each other in the blue and purple sections. Are they situated at the same angle as each other, or at opposite angles?

5) Are any of the strawberries sliced?

6) Is the watermelon closer to the limes or the zucchini?

Medium questions (3 points):

7) The rainbow runs diagonally from corner to corner. Which corner has the red produce?
   a) upper left
   b) upper right
   c) lower left
   d) lower right

8) How many bunches of bananas are there?

9) What is the best description of the group of tomatoes?
   a) about 10, attached together by their greenery in one batch
   b) about 10, attached together by their greenery in two batches
   c) over 15, attached together by their greenery in one batch
   d) over 15, attached together by their greenery in two batches

10) How many ears of corn are shown together?

Hard questions (5 points):

11) What is the third item from the top in the leftmost column?
    a) a group of red pears
    b) a pumpkin
    c) a purple-and-white cabbage
    d) a group of asparagus stalks

12) Looking at the picture as a whole, what is the correct order of these items from left to right?
    a) trio of red apples, trio of green apples, pair of yellow pears, broccoli
    b) trio of red apples, pair of yellow pears, broccoli, trio of green apples
    c) pair of yellow pears, trio of red apples, trio of green apples, broccoli
    d) pair of yellow pears, trio of green apples, broccoli, trio of red apples

Your score: _____
Maximum base score: 28
Answers, page 168

Easy questions (1 point):

1) Do we see the paying customer's right hand or left?

2) Are the woman's teeth visible?

3) What kind of objects appear on the woman's sweater?

4) On the wall on the left side of the photo, do the price tags appear on the clocks or on the dark green backing behind them?

5) Two thin diagonal beams are visible in the background space between the displays. Do they run from upper left to lower right, or from upper right to lower left?

6) One of the clocks has two straight, roughly parallel edges. Does this clock have a second hand?

Medium questions (3 points):

7) How many of the clocks that are visible in the scene use Roman numerals?

8) What color is the woman's headband?

9) What is the most notable thing about the clock face seen just to the left of the woman's outstretched hand?

10) What kind of motif borders the round clock at bottom left?

11) The variety of clock faces includes Arabic numerals, Roman numerals, and dots. Only one clock combines two of these. What is the pattern?
    a) dots on the inside ring; Roman numerals on the outside ring
    b) dots on the inside ring; Arabic numerals on the outside ring
    c) Roman numerals on the inside ring; dots on the outside ring
    d) Arabic numerals on the inside ring; dots on the outside ring

12) In the gap between the two displays of clocks, a round ornament can be seen hanging high on a hook. What color is it?

Hard questions (5 points):

13) Aside from a price tag, what can be seen in the large gap of the clock at the right?

14) How many wooden dowels are visible in the glass dish on the counter in front of the woman?

Your score: _____
Maximum base score: 34
Answers, page 168

Easy questions (1 point):

1) Is there a flag in the photo?

2) Is the teacher wearing a necktie or a bow tie?

3) On the blackboard, which way did the teacher write his numeral 1's?
   a) like this: l.
   b) like this: 1.

4) Is the teacher's hair parted on the side of his head that's in the photo, or on the other side?

Medium questions (3 points):

5) How many numbered sentences are written on the left side of the blackboard?

6) Approximately how many books are resting, edge down, on the teacher's desk?
   a) approximately 5
   b) approximately 10
   c) approximately 20

7) What object is resting on the far left edge of the desk?

8) What heading is written over the sentences?
   a) Sayings And Proverbs
   b) Proverbs And Sayings
   c) Sayings & Proverbs
   d) Proverbs & Sayings

Hard questions (5 points):

9) What is the first spelling word of the ten that are listed? (And for 5 extra points, what is the last?)

10) What is the longest proverb written on the board?

11) The spelling word "prescribe" is spelled incorrectly. How is it spelled?

Your score: _____
Maximum base score: 36
Answers, page 169

Easy questions (1 point):

1) Is any part of the street visible in the photograph?

2) Are any of the theater's doors open?

3) True or false: There is a garbage can at the street corner.

4) The large poster above the marquee in the left half of the picture is surrounded with white "Broadway lights." Does the marquee that stretches across the theater's façade have them as well?

Medium questions (3 points):

5) How many rows of red stars are on the long yellow sign between the doors?

6) What two colors are the woman's handbag?

7) What punctuation appears between the word "Beautiful" and the subtitle "The Carole King Musical"?
   a) none
   b) a period
   c) a colon
   d) an exclamation point

8) What is the name of the venue in this photograph?

9) Which of these surround the base of the tree in the photograph? (Choose all that apply.)
   a) fence
   b) dirt
   c) grass

10) The main image on the poster for this show is a smiling woman at a piano. How many times, in total, is that image seen in this photo?

Hard questions (5 points):

11) In the middle distance is somebody with their back to the camera seen with a bag. What color is the bag?

12) On the right, the yellow marquee has a repeating series of connected ribbons. How many droops are shown between the ribbons?

Your score: _____
Maximum base score: 32
Answers, page 169

44

Easy questions (1 point):

1) True or false: There is a window to the right of the double doors.

2) Is a flagpole visible on the roof of the town hall?

3) Which way does the wooden planking run on the building's front, vertically or horizontally?

4) On which side of the building is there a second step, left or right?

5) There is a diorama case on the porch in front of the large window. Does the case have a visible explanatory plaque?

Medium questions (3 points):

6) Which description of the sky in the photo is most accurate?
   a) gray clouds over the whole scene
   b) bright blue sky with a few wispy clouds
   c) a little blue sky on the left, gray clouds on the right

7) What item is on the porch's edge at the right side of the building?

8) Aside from the padlock on the door, what item in the scene is the most anachronistic, as it comes from an era more modern than the Old West?

9) What is most notable about the way the name of the building appears on the sign?

10) Which description of the view in the diorama is most accurate?
   a) desert landscape, cactus, low mountains in the distance
   b) gold rush town, horses, mountains in the distance
   c) artifacts including spurs, a bottle, and work gloves

Hard questions (5 points):

11) Which one of these years is not listed on the posted sign about Calico's population?
   a) 1881
   b) 1887
   c) 1890
   d) 1920
   e) 1951
   f) 1981
   g) 2081

12) The center post has two diagonal beams helping to support the canopy. How many similar angled beams does the support post on the left have?

13) How many spokes are around the hub on the wagon wheel seen in the distance on the photograph's right?
   a) 12
   b) 14
   c) 16

Your score: _____
Maximum base score: 35
Answers, page 169

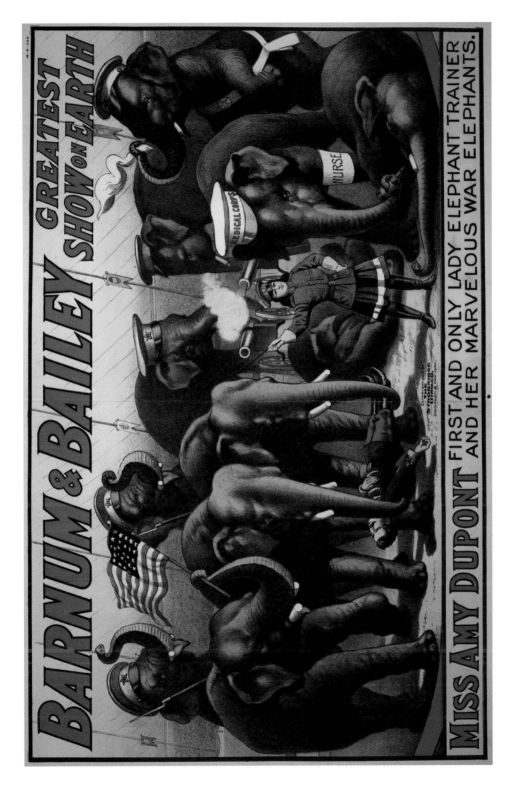

Easy questions (1 point):

1) What two colors are Miss Dupont's skirt?

2) Is Miss Dupont standing on a platform or the ground?

3) What color is the ampersand between the names Barnum and Bailey?
   a) red
   b) white
   c) blue

4) A man can be seen suspended between two of the elephants' trunks. Is he wearing a hat?

5) Which way does the American flag wave in the scene?
   a) from left to right
   b) from right to left

Medium questions (3 points):

6) What word is written on the armband of one of the elephants?

7) How many of the elephants are raising their trunks?
   a) one or two
   b) four or five
   c) seven

8) Does the description of Miss Amy Dupont along the bottom end with a period, an exclamation point, or no punctuation?

9) What word is used to describe Miss Amy Dupont's "war elephants"?
   a) stupendous
   b) marvelous
   c) trained

Hard questions (5 points):

10) What is the cause of the burst of smoke visible over Miss Dupont's head in the scene?

11) There are eleven elephants in the scene. How many are wearing a hat?

12) What kind of weapon can be seen at the far left?

Your score: _____
Maximum base score: 32
Answers, page 169

Easy questions (1 point):

1) True or false: All the boys are wearing long-sleeved shirts (although some have their sleeves rolled up).

2) Are any trees visible in the photo?

3) One boy is grasping the hand of another. Is the taller boy grasping the hand of the smaller boy, or is it the other way around?

4) In the background is a man riding a bicycle. Is he riding toward, or away from, the camera?

5) True or false: Every boy whose collar can be seen is wearing a tie.

6) The boy on the left is closest to the camera. On which side is his hair parted, his right or his left side?

Medium questions (3 points):

7) Approximately how many boys are looking into the camera?
   a) approximately 8
   b) approximately 10
   c) approximately 14

8) How many of the boys looking into the camera are wearing glasses?

9) A large tarp or awning is seen hanging on the right side of the photo, behind the boys. What color is it?

Hard questions (5 points):

10) One boy has his arms draped over the shoulders of two smaller boys. How many of the ears of those three boys are at all visible in the photo?
    a) 2
    b) 3
    c) 4
    d) 5
    e) 6

11) In the background is an advertisement with the word SAMSUNG. One of the letters is partially obscured by a pole. Which letter is it?

Your score: _____
Maximum base score: 25
Answers, page 169

Easy questions (1 point):

1) The high neon sign and the diner front render the diner's name differently from each other. Which one has a hyphen in the name "Rock-It"?

2) What is seen in silhouette against the colorful sky background?
   a) a city skyline
   b) a mountain
   c) a truck

3) Which kind of V shape do the diagonal metal bars on the two doors form—right side up or upside down?

4) On the high neon sign, does the rocket design have a red nose cone?

Medium questions (3 points):

5) Is the motorcycle parked to the left, in front, or to the right of the diner's entrance?

6) What colors, from left to right, are the four cars parked in front of the diner?
   a) turquoise, purple, yellow, red
   b) turquoise, purple, red, yellow
   c) turquoise, red, yellow, purple

7) How many windows does the front of the diner have (not including the entrance area)?

8) What time is indicated by the clock over the door?

9) Which phrase does not appear on the diner?
   a) Soda Fountain
   b) Open 24 Hours
   c) Home Cooking

10) How many of the cars are four-door?

11) The turquoise car has detailing in a second color. What color is it?

Hard questions (5 points):

12) How many of the cars have taillights that are round?

13) What can be seen inside the diner at the right end?

Your score: _____
Maximum base score: 35
Answers, page 169

Easy questions (1 point):

1) True or false: We can see the belt loops of the lead singer's pants

2) Does the electric cord pass in front of or behind the jumping guitarist on the right?

3) Are both of the drummer's hands visible?

4) Is the bassist on the left using his fingers or a pick?

5) The lead singer is wearing a wristband. Is it on the arm with the hand holding the microphone or the arm with the hand pointing in the air?

6) Do the pants of the bassist on the left have any holes at the knee?

Medium questions (3 points):

7) How many plaid shirts are in the scene?

8) Do we see the bottom surfaces of the cymbals, the tops, or a mix of both?

9) What kind of surface is the lead singer on?
a) tile floor
b) solid-colored mat
c) Oriental rug

10) There are several pillows on benches built into the back wall. What color is the lowest one?

Hard questions (5 points):

11) How many control knobs are there on the bass on the left?

12) The walls of the recording studio contain areas where sound buffers are clustered. How many such areas are visible?

Your score: _____
Maximum base score: 28
Answers, page 169

Easy questions (1 point):

1) True or false: The man with the top hat has a carnation in his lapel.

2) Does the curl on the forehead of the man on the left curl towards his own right ear or left ear?

3) Does the player on the right have more white or black chips showing?

4) There are two men in the background of the photo. Are they both seated?

5) Do the dog's ears stand up or flop down?

6) Does the handle on the beer mug on the left side of the table face left or right?

Medium questions (3 points):

7) How many of these players have sideburns?

8) Which one of the men seems to be drinking a glass of milk?

9) Which player is holding his cards with both hands?

10) How many cards can be seen lying on the table?

Hard questions (5 points):

11) How many playing cards are being held by the man in the middle?
    a) approximately 7
    b) approximately 10
    c) approximately 14

12) What is notable about the necktie of the man in the middle?

13) How many of buttons are visible on the dark coat hanging on the coathook?

Your score: _____
Maximum base score: 33
Answers, page 169

Easy questions (1 point):

1) Does the long handle that runs across the photo pass in front of or behind the candle?

2) Is the pocket watch's stem on the top or on the right side of the watch?

3) Is any of the candle's wick visible in the photo?

4) True or false: The pocket watch has a second hand.

5) Do the diagonal striations on the handle of the resting item run from upper left to lower right in the photo, or from upper right to lower left?

6) Is the Roman numeral for 4 on the watch face represented as IIII or IV?

7) Does a compass rose appear in the segment of the map seen in the photo?

Medium questions (3 points):

8) How is the XII on the watch different from the other Roman numerals?

9) What can be seen in the middle of the pocket watch?

10) What shape is the base of the candle holder?
    a) square
    b) round
    c) octagonal

11) What color is the candle?

Hard questions (5 points):

12) The watch face has three rings of numbers. How many of those rings have some numbers that are inverted so that the "bottom half" can be read face-up?

13) On the innermost ring of the watch face is a series of numbers that ends with 23. What number does it start with?

Your score: _____

Maximum base score: 29

Answers, page 169

Easy questions (1 point):

1) Do any of the stock traders have facial hair?

2) Is the man in front pointing with his right hand or his left?

3) True or false: There is a green number in the photo.

4) How many buttons are on the sleeve of the man in front?

Medium questions (3 points):

5) What color are the numbers in the last two columns?

6) As the trader in front holds his phone, how many of his visible fingers on the hand holding the phone are not touching it?

7) What color shirt is worn by the man with the receding hairline?

8) How many wedding rings are visible on the hands seen in the photo?

9) What number on the board in the background is highlighted in red?
   a) 54.49
   b) 45.59
   c) 54.94

10) How many open mouths can be seen in the photo?

11) What pattern is seen on the tie worn by the trader holding up his hand?
   a) stripes
   b) polka dots
   c) paisley
   d) none (it's a solid color)

Hard questions (5 points):

12) What percent is the smallest number seen on the board in the background?

13) What is notable about the way the trader holding up his hand is holding his phone?

Your score: _____
Maximum base score: 35
Answers, page 170

THE RULES FOR GOOD TEETH

3 Eat crisp foods that clean your teeth.

6 Visit your dentist regularly to keep your teeth healthy.

2 Rinse with water after meals to wash away sticky foods.

5 ...but eat fruit instead.

1 Brush your teeth after breakfast and last thing at night.

4 Don't eat sweet, sticky foods between meals...

REMEMBER – YOUR TEETH CAN'T LOOK AFTER THEMSELVES

By courtesy of The Oral Hygiene Service

Reduced monochrome reproduction of one of the coloured posters listed on page 18

Easy questions (1 point):

1) What is the name of this page?
   a) The Rules for Clean Teeth
   b) The Rules for Healthy Teeth
   c) The Rules for Good Teeth

2) Are there any teeth shown in this picture?

3) True or false: The dentist is wearing glasses.

4) Is the number 4 represented with an open top or a pointed top?

5) In the picture where the boy is holding his toothbrush in one hand and toothpaste in the other, which item is held higher?

6) The girl's collar has a ruffle. Does the end of her sleeve have one?

7) Do the characters' hands have four fingers and a thumb, or three fingers and a thumb?

8) Do the numbers under each picture have periods after them?

Medium questions (3 points):

9) Complete this phrase that appears at the bottom: Remember—your teeth …
   a) can't take care of themselves
   b) can't look after themselves
   c) can't do it on their own

10) In the drawing of crisp foods, what kind of vegetable is highlighted in white?

11) How many candies appear in picture 4?

12) According to the panel with the girl, why should you rinse with water after meals?

13) What is the dentist holding?
    a) a tube of toothpaste
    b) a dental mirror
    c) a toothbrush

14) How many of the girl's ears are showing?

Hard questions (5 points):

15) What does the caption for picture 4 say that the boy with the bandage shouldn't eat between meals?
    a) sweet, sticky foods
    b) chewy, sticky candy
    c) sticky sweets

16) How many times does the word "smile" appear on the page?

17) What article of clothing is missing from the boy in one picture that he is wearing in his other two pictures?

Your score: _____
Maximum base score: 41
Answers, page 170

Easy questions (1 point):

1) True or false: All of the costumed people are wearing hats.

2) Does any part of the costumed woman on the left's salmon-colored dress touch the ground?

3) There is an explanatory plaque with two columns of type posted along the edge of the path. Which column has more lines of type?

4) Is the man wearing the modern necktie in a long-sleeved or short-sleeved shirt?

5) The gateposts in the scene are topped with diamond shapes. Are the top pieces of the diamonds longer than the bottom ones, or are the bottom pieces longer than the top ones?

Medium questions (3 points):

6) How many people in the scene are taking pictures?

7) What kind of item is leaning against the wall at the far right edge of the photo?

8) What are the observers in the background standing on?
   a) cobblestones
   b) gravel
   c) grass

9) How many people in the scene are facing away from the camera?

Hard questions (5 points):

10) On how many of the costumed men can we see white leggings?

11) The man nearest the camera is holding a walking stick in his left hand. Where is his right hand?

12) Behind the costumed woman in the salmon-colored dress stand seven costumed people in a row, including one woman. Counting from the left of the scene, what number is that second woman?

13) What color is the coat of the first costumed man in that row, the one farthest to the left?

Your score: _____
Maximum base score: 37
Answers, page 170

Easy questions (1 point):

1) True or false: The label of the record on the left is red.

2) Which of the two curved tone arms visible on the gramophones in the photograph has a brass-colored section?

3) Does the clock in the middle have Roman numerals or Arabic numerals?

4) Do the two gramophone horns divided into sections have the same number of sections as each other?

5) Are the two visible turntables (the platters that hold and rotate the records) wider than the records?

Medium questions (3 points):

6) What color is the crank handle on the gramophone on the left?

7) What time is shown on the black clock in the middle of the photograph?

a) approximately 8:29
b) approximately 9:29
c) approximately 5:44
d) approximately 6:44

8) The cat-shaped statuette on the right has a colorful design on its back. What two colors are the beads affixed on this design?

9) The gramophone on the left has a design of raised silver squares on the front of its table. How many of those squares run all the way from left to right across the top?

a) 12
b) 16
c) 20

Hard questions (5 points):

10) What is notable about the tilted clock face visible at the lower right side of the photograph?

11) Each section of the gramophone horn on the left has a row of dots at the outer rim. How many dots are in each section?

12) The tilted clock at the lower right is obscured by other objects. Which one of these numbers on the clock face is not visible in the photograph?

a) 4
b) 7
c) 9

Your score: _____
Maximum base score: 32
Answers, page 170

Easy questions (1 point):

1) True or false: One of the kitchen cabinets is open.

2) As the man enters the house, is the open door on his left side or his right?

3) Are the woman's pants tucked into her boots?

4) Does the countertop on the kitchen island have square or rounded edges?

5) Are both the man's feet inside the home, or is he stepping over the threshold?

6) Under the counter are two red stools. Can we see all of the flat sitting surface of both stools?

Medium questions (3 points):

7) What color is the filing box held by the woman?

8) Which best describes what the man in the photo is wearing?
   a) a buttoned long-sleeved shirt with the sleeves rolled up
   b) an unbuttoned long-sleeved shirt over a T-shirt
   c) a light zippered jacket over a T-shirt

9) How many recessed lights are visible, in whole or in part, in the ceiling over the kitchen area?

10) Do the kitchen cabinets open with handles, knobs, or neither?

11) How are the refrigerator doors in the scene arranged?
   a) side by side
   b) freezer door on top
   c) freezer door on bottom

12) Aside from boxes and the briefcase, what other item is on the kitchen island?

Hard questions (5 points):

13) There is a cardboard box on the floor. Which of these describes the box most closely?
   a) it is open and we can see all four flaps
   b) it is closed in a cloverleaf-type arrangement, each flap on top of the next
   c) the two outer flaps are visible but they are not sealed
   d) the two outer flaps are sealed with tape

14) What pattern appears on the tissue box near the kettle?

Your score: _____
Maximum base score: 34
Answers, page 170

69

Easy questions (1 point):

1) True or false: The woman's apron features a pattern of cupcakes.

2) Does the shadow cast by the wooden spoons in the bowl extend to the side of the refrigerator?

3) Which foot is the woman holding farther forward, her left or her right?

4) Is the woman wearing earrings?

Medium questions (3 points):

5) How many ice trays are visible on the highest shelf in the freezer?

6) What kind of motif is on the window curtain?

7) How much of the milk bottle is filled?
   a) it appears to be unopened
   b) somewhat more than half
   c) somewhat less than half
   d) just a little

8) How many drawer and cabinet handles are visible to the left of the refrigerator?

9) What word appears on each of the two drawers at the bottom of the refrigerator?

Hard questions (5 points):

10) What type of design is on the end of the loaf of Tip-Top bread?
    a) stars
    b) stripes
    c) balloons
    d) paraders

11) What item is on the counter behind the refrigerator door?

12) Place these items in order by the shelves they are on, from top to bottom: Tip-Top bread, eggs, platter of dessert cups with whipped cream, Canada Dry bottle

Your score: _____
Maximum base score: 34
Answers, page 170

Easy questions (1 point):

1) Do the wooden planks in the background run horizontally or vertically?

2) Does the pumpkin with the largest set of teeth have any missing teeth?

3) Which part of the pile of pumpkins is tallest: the left side, the middle, or the right side?

4) Does the large gourd on the left with a floppy top still have its stem?

5) One of the pumpkins has a mouth carved to look like stitches. Is this pumpkin smiling or frowning?

6) Does the face of the large, round, grimacing pumpkin in the middle have a nose?

Medium questions (3 points):

7) How many pumpkins are shown?
   a) 15
   b) 20
   c) 25

8) Are the pumpkins resting on light wood, dark wood, or is the surface not shown?

9) What type of line is carved around the lid of each pumpkin?

10) What is resting on the face of the heavily tilted pumpkin at the top middle?

11) How many of the pumpkins have holes carved out to represent eyebrows?
    a) none
    b) one
    c) three

Hard questions (5 points):

12) What is distinct about the smiling pumpkin tilted to the right on the right side of the photo?

13) How many teeth does the pumpkin at the far right have?

Your score: _____
Maximum base score: 31
Answers, page 170

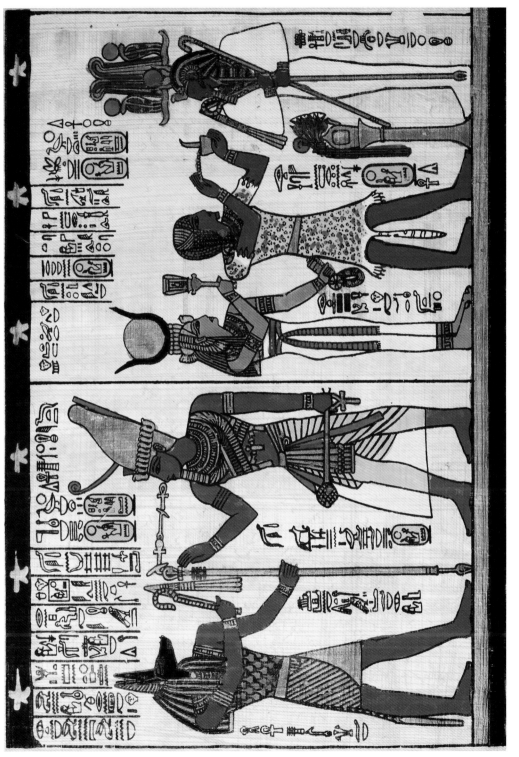

Easy questions (1 point):

1) Does the figure at the left, with the animal head, have its mouth open or closed?

2) Within the rows of hieroglyphs are some outlined tablets, known as cartouches. What color are they? Bonus question for 1 point: How many pairs of adjacent cartouches are there?

3) Does the left or right half of this scene contain the hieroglyphs that go closest to the bottom of the image?

4) Is the ear of the tallest figure visible?

Medium questions (3 points):

5) How many star-shaped symbols run along the top of the image?

6) Of the five large figures in the scene, how many face left?

7) What color are the circles on the headpiece atop the figure at far right?

8) The upper-left column of hieroglyphics contains two of what kind of animal?
   a) bird
   b) rabbit
   c) snake

9) How many of the figures are wearing a see-through article of clothing?

10) What is seen at the bottom of the yellow and red article of clothing?

Hard questions (5 points):

11) Do the fibers visible in the papyrus upon which these images were rendered run horizontally, vertically, or both?

12) How many of the ten hands seen in the image are not holding something?

13) Besides the feet of the main figures, how many other objects are resting on the floor in the scene?

Your score: _____
Maximum base score: 38
Answers, page 170

Easy questions (1 point):

1) Can anybody be seen hailing a cab?

2) Are the two gray sedans two-door or four-door vehicles?

3) Can any trees be seen in the photograph?

4) Does either lamppost in the scene have a traffic sign affixed to it?

Medium questions (3 points):

5) According to the digital display, what time is it?

6) How many flags are grouped at the left of the scene?

7) What company's logo and name appears to the left and right of the words PENN STATION?

8) What is the taxi code on top of the taxi at the left?
   a) 747P
   b) 74P7
   c) 7P74

9) According to the blue street sign in the distance, what number is the cross street?

10) How many styles of license plate can be seen in the photo?

Hard questions (5 points):

11) Which letter of MADISON SQUARE GARDEN is obscured by the lamppost?

12) Atop the roof of the building's entrance is an ad for a radio program. When can it be heard?

13) How many Chase Bank logos are visible in the scene?

Your score: _____
Maximum base score: 37
Answers, page 170

Easy questions (1 point):

1) What two colors are on the tent hanging over the jousting scene?

2) The jousters are separated by a series of railings. How many horizontal bars does each of these railings have?
   a) one
   b) two

3) Does the helmet of either jouster have a raised visor?

4) What season do the trees in the background indicate?
   a) summer
   b) fall

5) On the lance nearest the camera, do the red and white stripes run from upper left to lower right, or from lower left to upper right?

Medium questions (3 points):

6) Compared to the railing, how is the nearest lance positioned in the photograph?
   a) pointing down towards the railing
   b) pointing up, away from the railing
   c) parallel with the railing

7) How many of the front horse's lower legs are covered for protection?

8) What is the surface that the horses are being ridden on?
   a) sand
   b) dirt
   c) grass

9) Approximately how many of the spectators on the right are standing behind the seated crowd?
   a) approximately 10
   b) approximately 15
   c) approximately 20

Hard questions (5 points):

10) A coat of arms hangs from the roof of the covered structure in the background. What two colors make up that coat of arms?

11) In the background is a woman in gray on the steps of the covered structure. What is she holding?

12) The near horse is wearing a covering of red, yellow, and black over its back. What is the far horse wearing?
    a) a covering similar to the one on the near horse
    b) black leather straps with studs
    c) a blue and yellow covering

Your score: _____
Maximum base score: **32**
Answers, page 171

Easy questions (1 point):

1) True or false: An American flag can be seen somewhere in the photo.

2) In the framed portrait on the back wall, does the subject face to our left or right?

3) Is the woman on the stand sitting in an enclosed or an open witness box?

4) Do the chairs that the jury is sitting in have arms?

5) Against the back wall is a tall door. Does it have a transom window?

6) At a table on the left side of the scene is a man writing something. Is he left-handed or right-handed?

Medium questions (3 points):

7) Against the back wall of the scene are four men and one woman. Counting from the left, which number is the woman?

8) The jury contains a young man whose face can be seen in profile. Which one of these is not part of his description?
   a) sideburns
   b) glasses
   c) mustache
   d) goatee

9) What shape are the two lamps above the judge's head?

Hard questions (5 points):

10) How many of the judge's hands are visible in the photo?

11) What is notable about the eyewear worn by the judge?

12) How many members of the jury are seen wearing hats?

Your score: _____
Maximum base score: 30
Answers, page 171

Easy questions (1 point):

1) True or false: The hair of the player shooting the ball is in a ponytail.

2) Is the jersey of the player shooting the ball tucked into her waistband, or untucked?

3) Is the person operating the camera in the background a man or a woman?

4) Which of the shooter's hands is touching the ball?

5) Are all four players' sneakers the same color?

6) How does the number 4 appear on the jersey in the photograph, with an open 4 or a closed one (forming a triangle inside)?

Medium questions (3 points):

7) Two players' names are partially visible. What are the first letters of each? (Give yourself 1 point if you get one correct but not both.)

8) What school do the players wearing white represent?

9) What is the uniform number of the player shooting the ball?

10) The leftmost of the people sitting on the floor is holding something in his right hand. What is it?

11) What is visible on the lower right of the backboard?
a) a Nike logo
b) a Staples logo
c) an American flag
d) nothing

Hard questions (5 points):

12) What is the sum of the uniform numbers of the two players in white?

13) Single-letter team logos appear on the players' shorts. List all the visible letters, from left to right in the photo.

14) How many of the players' eight feet are touching the ground?

Your score: _____
Maximum base score: 36
Answers, page 171

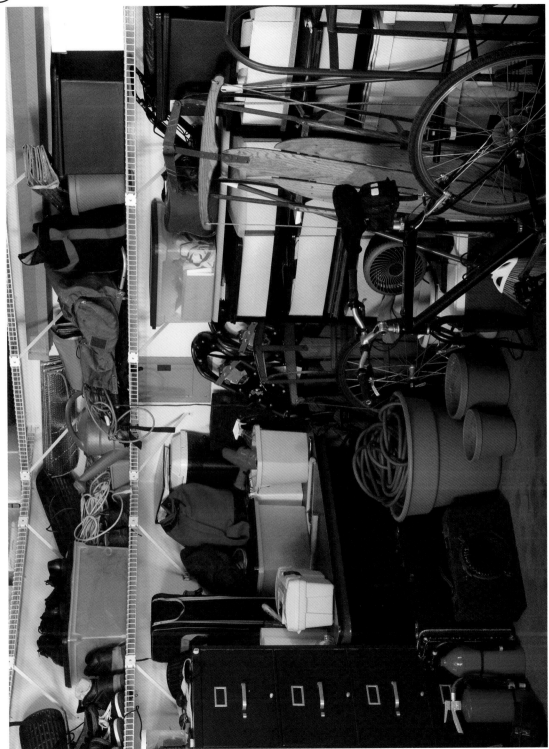

Easy questions (1 point):

1) Are the two electrical cords on the same shelf or is one on a higher shelf than the other?

2) Is the garden hose's nozzle visible in the photo?

3) True or false: There are a pair of skis in the photo.

4) Is the blue plastic watering can situated so that its spout faces to the left or the right?

5) Does the tall sled on the right side have writing on it?

Medium questions (3 points):

6) What color is the toolbox on the table just to the right of the filing cabinet?

7) There are two similar red items on the floor just in front of the filing cabinet. What are both of those items?

8) How many terra cotta pots are visible in the picture?

9) What is the main color of the cooler on the floor behind the bicycle?

10) What is most notable about the bicycle's front tire?

11) There is a broom in the photo whose bristles are split into two sections. What colors are those two sections?

Hard questions (5 points):

12) What is the looseleaf binder resting on?

13) What is the only thing visible on the wall behind the stuff?

Your score: _____
Maximum base score: 33
Answers, page 171

Easy questions (1 point):

1) True or false: The cereals are all made by the same company.

2) Do any of the cereal logos have lowercase letters in their names?

3) Is the box of Corn Pops in the top row or the bottom row?

Medium questions (3 points):

4) Which two cereals appear twice?

5) How is the word "Great" spelled on the box of Frosted Flakes?
   a) Grrreat!
   b) Gr-r-reat!
   c) Grr-reat!

6) Of the three characters wearing hats that say Snap, Crackle, and Pop, which has a striped hat?

7) Which is the only box that shows a spoon?

8) Which two cereals are a good source of vitamin D? Give yourself 3 points for each one.

9) The Corn Flakes box shows a rooster logo with three tail feathers. What colors are the tail feathers, from top to bottom?
   a) green, yellow, red
   b) yellow, green, red
   c) red, yellow, green

10) How many of the words in the cereal names are written in red (not counting "Kellogg's")?

11) Which is the only box that does not say how many calories are inside?

12) Which one of these words does not appear on the Corn Pops box?
    a) Crispy
    b) Puffed
    c) Crunchy
    d) Glazed
    e) Sweet

Hard questions (5 points):

13) What appears on the end of the large ampersand on the tops of the Froot Loops and Apple Jacks boxes?

14) In the Froot Loops logo, what colors are the O's in "Loops"?
    a) blue and yellow
    b) green and yellow
    c) green and purple

15) Which cereal's box has the greatest net weight?

16) What color stripe is immediately to the left of the black end of the toucan's beak?

Your score: _____
Maximum base score: 53
Answers, page 171

Easy questions (1 point):

1) One of the standing girls has her hand to her lip. Is it her right or left hand?

2) On the wall near the lower right corner of some of the paintings is an image of earphones. Is the image under or to the right of the corner?

3) True or false: The woman with the outstretched arm is wearing a ring.

4) Does the portrait of the woman with an exposed shoulder have an interior or exterior background?

Medium questions (3 points):

5) Over the gallery entrance is a bar with two colors. What are the two colors?

6) There are three adults standing behind the seated kids. One of them is wearing glasses. Where is that adult?
a) on the left
b) in the middle
c) on the right

7) How many paintings can be seen hanging on the main wall in the photograph?

8) There is a standing girl with a flowery top and red sneakers. What word appears on her shirt?

Hard questions (5 points):

9) What color top is worn by the woman standing at the far left, under the entrance to the gallery?

10) What kind of animals can be seen in the background in the largest painting?

11) How many total bonnets appear in the paintings?

12) What color is the top of the bench the children are sitting on?

Your score: _____
Maximum base score: 36
Answers, page 171

Easy questions (1 point):

1) True or false: The man sitting on the bench is doing curls with his left arm.

2) Which is the spotter for the woman on the bench press wearing, sweatpants or shorts?

3) Does the person on the treadmill wearing the green top have the left or the right leg farther back?

4) Are socks visible on the woman on the bench press?

5) Does the long hair of the woman in the background extend below the bottom of her sports bra?

6) True or false: The spotter for the woman on the bench press has a tattoo on one of his arms.

Medium questions (3 points):

7) What color are the tips of the metal legs of the bench press on the floor?

8) How many holes are cut into each of the large yellow weights (not including the center hole)?
a) 7
b) 8
c) 9

9) How many blank placards appear on the pillar on the right side of the scene?

10) For the three people on the treadmills, what color are their tops from left to right?
a) green, red, black
b) green, black, red
c) red, green, black
d) red, black, green
e) black, red, green
f) black, green, red

Hard questions (5 points):

11) How many wristwatches are visible in the scene?

12) Of the three people with their backs to us, how many of their reflections are visible in the mirror?

Your score: _____
Maximum base score: 28
Answers, page 171

Easy questions (1 point):

1) True or false: The paraders are all walking with the same foot forward.

2) Is there a street sign visible in the photo?

3) Does the high window over the ornate church entrance in the distance have a balcony?

4) Are the drummers wearing their strap over their left or right shoulder?

5) True or false: Each cape has a fringe that matches the color of the cape.

6) There is a church name written on the wall the paraders are marching past. Are any of the letters accented?

Medium questions (3 points):

7) What color, along with black, runs around the edge of the drum held by the drummer on the left?

8) What logo is visible on the white shopping bag held by one of the observers?
   a) Museu del Prado
   b) Museu Picasso
   c) Sagrada Família

9) A woman with her hair in a ponytail and her hands in her coat pocket is watching the parade. What is she wearing on her feet?

10) What color flag is highest in the photograph?

Hard questions (5 points):

11) What two surfaces are the paraders walking on?
    a) large paving stones and cobblestones
    b) black asphalt and cobblestones
    c) large paving stones and black asphalt

12) What is notable about the wrists of the drummers, most visible on the right wrist of the drummer at the left?

Your score: _____
Maximum base score: 28
Answers, page 171

Easy questions (1 point):

1) Is the door in the background open or closed?

2) Are any of the strings of pearls worn in the picture knotted?

3) True or false: The carpet is a solid color.

4) Is the bride holding her flowers toward, or away from, the woman in the mink?

5) The man in the scene is wearing a tie with diagonal stripes. On the tie's knot, which way do the stripes go: from upper left to lower right, or from upper right to lower left?

Medium questions (3 points):

6) There is a painting on the wall in the background. What kind of frame does it have?
   a) a simple rectangular frame
   b) a rectangular frame with an oval mat
   c) an oval frame

7) How many of the people in the photograph are looking at the bride?

8) What is the man holding?

9) What is the shape of the tabletop on the left?
   a) rectangular
   b) oval
   c) round

10) How many of the people in the photograph are holding flowers?

Hard questions (5 points):

11) What is the only kind of jewelry visible on the kneeling woman?

12) How many strings of pearls are seen around the neck of the woman standing behind the kneeling woman?

Your score: _____
Maximum base score: 30
Answers, page 172

Easy questions (1 point):

1) True or false: The person in blue walking in the center of the scene is wearing a backpack.

2) Are any flowers visible in the photograph?

3) There is a pipe that runs vertically down the brick wall over the Pandora store, where it then turns and continues. Does it turn toward the left or the right?

4) At the top right is a sign with an ampersand. Is it a closed ampersand, or one that looks like a rounded capital E?

5) Is the person with the blue polka-dotted bag wearing the bag over the left or right shoulder?

Medium questions (3 points):

6) A shaft of sunlight can be seen shining through, at the right. How many people are standing in the sunlight?

7) What three items are touted just after Pandora's store name?
a) Toys, Games & Souvenirs
b) Gifts, Games & Chocolate
c) Games, Gifts & Souvenirs

8) What items are being sold on the sidewalk below the rack of postcards?

9) On the left side of the street, the shop window to the right of the door has a sign over it on which a single word is written in red capital letters. What is that word?

10) How much do souvenir T-shirts cost, according to the Pandora window display?

Hard questions (5 points):

11) How many panes is the Pandora window display on the left divided into?
a) 36 (nine columns by four rows)
b) 32 (eight columns by four rows)
c) 27 (nine columns by three rows)
d) 18 (six columns by three rows)

12) What is the main color of the windowframe that can be seen behind the man in the suit?

13) How many stories tall is the building in the distance (the building that the alley seems to point toward)?

Your score: _____
Maximum base score: 35
Answers, page 172

Easy questions (1 point):

1) True or false: There are no numbers showing on the screen of the calculator.

2) Which of the Post-it pads is on top, the blue or the olive?

3) Do the grid lines in the graph paper notebook go to the edges of the page, or is there a border?

4) Is any part of a computer visible in the photograph?

5) Is the pocket clip on the mechanical pencil that's resting on the blank page facing left or right?

6) Are the glasses resting completely on the graph paper?

Medium questions (3 points):

7) What color is the smaller metal alligator clip, which is attached to the edge of a file folder?

8) The top Post-it pad is positioned with the adhesive surface in which of these locations?
   a) at the top
   b) at the bottom
   c) on the left side
   d) on the right side

9) Part of a glass is showing at the top of the photograph. We can tell what's in it because of the shadows cast. What does it contain? And for a bonus point, how many of the shadows are on the left-hand page of the notebook?

10) In the stack of papers a stripe of color can be seen on the left side. What color is the stripe?

Hard questions (5 points):

11) Toward which other object in the photo does the coffee mug's handle most closely point?
   a) toward the balled-up piece of paper
   b) toward the rubber band ball
   c) toward the calculator
   d) toward the Post-it pads

12) On the calculator, what two letters appear on the narrow button at the upper right corner?

Your score: _____
Maximum base score: 29
Answers, page 172

Easy questions (1 point):

1) True or false: The ballerina is wearing a tiara.

2) Are the leggings (from the knees up) worn by the tin soldiers red or white?

3) Is there any fake snow on the stage floor?

4) Is the bow on the ballerina's dress at her chest or her waist?

5) Does the cape worn by the leaning man touch the ground?

6) Does the prince's costume have epaulets on the shoulders?

Medium questions (3 points):

7) The soldier behind the prince is holding two gold swords. What colors are their handles?
   a) both gold
   b) one gold, one red
   c) both red

8) With her right hand, the ballerina holds the hand of the prince. Is her left arm raised, out to her side, or down?

9) What color are the manes on the hobbyhorses?

10) Approximately how many foil stars, representing ornaments, are visible against the scenery?
    a) approximately 3
    b) approximately 6
    c) approximately 9

Hard questions (5 points):

11) What is notable about the hat worn by the tin soldier at far right?

12) Of the three central figures, how many of them have their heels off the ground?

13) There are three hobbyhorses being held in the photograph. Which way do their heads face?
    a) all three to the right
    b) all three to the left
    c) two to the right and one to the left
    d) two to the left and one to the right

Your score: _____
Maximum base score: 33
Answers, page 172

Easy questions (1 point):

1) True or false: The icons you can see in the small game at the top left all appear in the main large game as well.

2) Which appears higher, the horseshoe or the sun?

3) Are the rainbow's colors accurate?

Medium questions (3 points):

4) What color is the coin being held?

5) What complete playing card is shown as one of the icons?

6) What is the highest prize amount clearly shown? For 3 extra points, what is the lowest?

7) Give yourself 3 points for every one of the three red fruit icons shown that you can name.

8) What word appears on the coin icon?

9) What color is the large X that marks the diagonals?

10) What living creatures appear on the ticket?
    a) bird, cat, ladybug
    b) cat, ladybug, elephant
    c) elephant, ladybug, bird

11) What is the game number of the large game?

12) What is the icon in the center of the large game?

13) One icon shows an identical pair of dice. How many pips are on the top of each die?

Hard questions (5 points):

14) What is the prize amount for the middle column?

15) Which of these best describes the background of the ticket?
    a) swirly yellow and brown stripes
    b) straight purple and yellow stripes
    c) diagonal yellow and white stripes

Your score: _____
Maximum base score: 52
Answers, page 172

Easy questions (1 point):

1) True or false: There is a clock on the mantelpiece.

2) Is there a skylight in the ceiling?

3) At the left of the photo is an entrance to another part of the lodge. Is there a painting hanging over that entrance?

4) Do the two beams on the ceiling run parallel to each other or do they meet at the ceiling's peak?

Medium questions (3 points):

5) Behind the large sofa on the right is a table. What can be seen under the table?
a) a plant
b) spare firewood
c) a stack of snowshoes

6) What color is the ceramic pot on the mantelpiece?

7) At the far right of the scene is a carved wooden dresser with three drawers. Which drawer is embellished with a large wood carving?
a) the top
b) the middle
c) the bottom

8) What is in the center of the coffee table at the center of the scene?

9) There is a blanket on one of the sofas in the scene. Where is it located?
a) over the left side of the two-seater
b) over the right side of the two-seater
c) on the far end of the large sofa
d) on the near end of the large sofa

10) What kind of animal is silhouetted on the lamp near the center of the photograph?

Hard questions (5 points):

11) What is notable about the rivets on the side of the large sofa and the easy chair?

12) How many ceiling fan blades are visible?

13) How many circular light fixtures can be seen in the ceiling outside the window on the upper level?

Your score: _____
Maximum base score: 37
Answers, page 172

Easy questions (1 point):

1) True or false: The rodeo rider is holding the frayed rope attached to the horse.

2) Are the rider's pants tucked into his boots?

3) Can we see any part of the horse's tail?

4) The man standing on the right side of the ring holding the red and white striped rope is wearing a hat. Is it the same color hat as the one that the rider is wearing?

Medium questions (3 points):

5) What color is the horse's mane?
   a) black
   b) white
   c) brown

6) What is the website in the ad for Nebraska?
   a) SeeNebraska.com
   b) ComeToNebraska.com
   c) VisitNebraska.com

7) What is written on the strap across the horse's muzzle?

8) There are two men wearing identical outfits who are standing in the ring. Both wear jeans; which of the following best describes the rest of their outfits?
   a) plaid shirts, tan vests
   b) solid-colored shirts, tan vests
   c) plaid shirts, blue vests
   d) solid-colored shirts, blue vests

Hard questions (5 points):

9) What color are the seat backs of the row of unoccupied seats in the stands?

10) There is a woman with a bright yellow outfit in the stands. Where are her hands?
    a) in the air
    b) out in front of her
    c) holding a camera to her face
    d) cupping her face
    e) gripping the railing in front of her

11) Where does the word "rodeo" appear in the photograph?

Your score: _____
Maximum base score: 31
Answers, page 172

Easy questions (1 point):

1) True or false: All five people are holding their phones in their right hands.

2) Are any of the people crossing their ankles?

3) One person's pant legs are rolled up. One person's pant legs have holes at the knees. Are these two different people, or the same person?

4) Is the light blue phone held by a man or a woman?

5) True or false: None of the women's ears are visible.

6) There is a bicycle in the background of the scene. Does it face right or left?

Medium questions (3 points):

7) How many of the people in the scene are wearing hats?

8) What color are the pants of the woman in the middle?

9) How many levels of metal rails are visible below the surface the five people are sitting on?

10) What item is sitting next to the person at the far right?

11) How many of the people are resting part of their feet on the top metal rail?

Hard questions (5 points):

12) Numbered from left to right, which people in the scene have scarves?

13) What color is the awning over the window in the background at the far right?

14) How many of the people have footwear with laces?

15) What is notably different about the way the woman on the left is holding her phone?

Your score: _____
Maximum base score: 41
Answers, page 172

Easy questions (1 point):

1) True or false: Of the couples dancing together, the men are all on the right side in the photo.

2) Does the band include a guitarist?

3) Of the couple at the front center of the scene, which of the woman's knees is all the way forward, her left or her right?

4) Do the streamers that hang from the ceiling all the way across the room pass in front of, or behind, the hanging chandelier?

5) Is the floor made of the same planking as the walls?

Medium questions (3 points):

6) Of the women in the front, how many can be seen to be completely off their feet?

7) Approximately how many band members can be seen on the raised platform?
   a) approximately 12
   b) approximately 15
   c) approximately 18

8) The bunting hanging on the sides of the room contains three shades of stripe. Is the darkest shade at the top, middle, or bottom?

9) How many lanterns are hanging from the wooden chandelier at the center of the photo?

Hard questions (5 points):

10) A woman in suspenders is leaning backward a bit to the left of the photo's center. Of her free hand, which of her fingers is/are pointing toward the ceiling?
    a) her index and middle fingers (a "V" sign)
    b) her index finger and pinkie
    c) only her pinkie
    d) only her index finger

11) A young woman in a light-colored dress can be seen on the right side of the photo, leaning against something. What is it?

12) To the center right is a tall couple joined by their outstretched hands. Which hands are they joining?
    a) both near hands (those closest to the camera)
    b) both far hands (those farthest from the camera)
    c) one of each hand (reaching across their bodies)

Your score: _____
Maximum base score: 32
Answers, page 173

Easy questions (1 point):

1) Is the gravy boat pointed toward or away from the turkey?

2) Of the dishes with the cranberry sauce and the Brussels sprouts, only one has a utensil. Which one?

3) Which is nearer the turkey, the salt or the pepper?

4) Is the asparagus arranged so that the tips are on the left or right side of their plate?

5) The table has a cloth runner down its center. Is the carving knife resting on or off the runner?

Medium questions (3 points):

6) What two colors are the flowers on the table?

7) What kind of food is on the small rectangular plate in the front?

8) How many miniature pumpkins or gourds are visible in the photograph?

9) What else is on the platter with the asparagus?

10) What shape is the platter holding the turkey?

11) How many candles are in the photograph?

Hard questions (5 points):

12) Approximately how many cranberries are on the same platter as the turkey?
    a) approximately 10
    b) approximately 15
    c) approximately 25

13) What is unusual about the dish holding the breadcrumb stuffing at the left?

Your score: _____
Maximum base score: 33
Answers, page 173

Easy questions (1 point):

1) The white building has two spires. Which is taller, the one on the left or the right?

2) Are any of the toy cars in the exhibit yellow taxicabs?

3) In the clock tower on the red building, approximately what time is it?
   a) approximately 4:00
   b) approximately 7:00
   c) approximately 9:30

4) True or false: The Lego logo can be seen backward in a reflection somewhere in the glass.

5) Is the "floor" of the exhibit made of Lego bricks or is it a painted platform?

6) There is a red toy car to the right of the covered commuters. Is it facing left or right?

Medium questions (3 points):

7) Which two of these three items are seen in the display?
   a) a hot air balloon
   b) a roller coaster
   c) a snowy mountain

8) The train car closest to the front is a flatcar that's carrying a shipping container. What are the colors of the shipping container?

9) Of the pillars holding up the façade of the Federalist-style building, how many make up the front row?
   a) 5
   b) 8
   c) 10

10) Running across the background is a bar of color that is the top of the store's display shelves. What color is this bar?

Hard questions (5 points):

11) A series of similar items can be seen near the store's ceiling, outside the glass case. What are they?

12) The man on the right, seen through the glass, has three stripes at the end of his sleeve. What colors are they?

Your score: _____
Maximum base score: 28
Answers, page 173

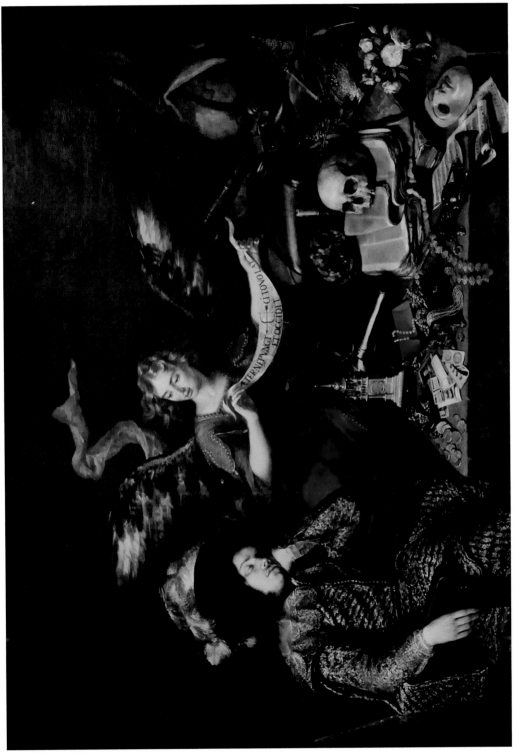

Easy questions (1 point):

1) Is there a glow behind the head of the angel?

2) Is the sleeping figure wearing a ring on the hand that's showing?

3) True or false: The skull sitting on the book is missing its lower jaw.

4) Which is higher in the painting: the globe or the angel's wings?

5) Is the angel lifting either pinkie?

6) Are the ends of the chair's arms blunt or rounded?

7) Is a musical instrument among the array of items?

Medium questions (3 points):

8) How many columns of type can be seen on each page of the book?

9) What color is the lining inside the jewelry box's lid?

10) What image is depicted in the middle of the banner held by the angel?

11) Approximately how many coins are shown spilled near the edge of the table?
   a) approximately 10
   b) approximately 15
   c) approximately 25

12) What is the main color of the miniature building in front of the angel?

Hard questions (5 points):

13) What is notable about the capital I's on the banner?

14) Place these items in order from left to right on the table: candle, flowers, jewelry box, mask.

Your score: _____
Maximum base score: 32
Answers, page 173

Easy questions (1 point):

1) The pink sign has many words only partially visible. Can all of the word SAVED be seen?

2) Two women can be seen wearing earrings. Are they hoops or studs?

3) There are two people in the scene looking toward the photographer. Are they men or women?

Medium questions (3 points):

4) Besides the red circle with the line through it, what are two other symbols seen somewhere on the protest signs?
a) "at" sign and star
b) "at" sign and dollar sign
c) star and ampersand
d) dollar sign and ampersand

5) Besides white, what color sign appears most often?

6) What words are in the red circle with the slash through it?

7) What, if anything, can be seen in the background beyond the protesters?
a) buildings
b) trees
c) the protesters fill the scene

8) A large sign near the center calls for unity among what group of people?

9) One man in the crowd can be seen wearing a wristband. What color is this band?

10) Which one of these is written on a sign using lowercase letters, after an initial capital letter?
a) Life
b) Support
c) Violence

Hard questions (5 points):

11) There is a man with a mustache and beard at the far right edge of the photo. In the word visible on his shirt, what are the doubled letters?

12) One sign maker used a different color for each letter of a word. What are the four letters we can see of that word?

Your score: _____
Maximum base score: 34
Answers, page 173

Easy questions (1 point):

1) Do the cars have visible license plates?

2) True or false: The two blue cars are identical models.

3) The back wall is made of wooden planking. Does the planking run vertically or horizontally?

4) Are there any whitewall tires visible in the photo?

5) The green car at the left is painted in two tones, a lighter and darker shade of green. Is the hood of the car primarily the lighter or the darker shade?

6) The nearer blue car has a two-pane windshield. Is the placard there posted on the left or the right pane, from the viewer's perspective?

Medium questions (3 points):

7) There are three round objects hanging in a straight vertical line on the back wall above the green car. What color are they?

8) How many vertical green beams can be seen on the back wall?

9) What word appears in blue under the word GULF on the sign hanging overhead?
a) OIL
b) GAS
c) DEALER

10) Of the door handles on the nearer blue car, are they both on the left end of the doors, both on the right, or are they near each other at the center?

11) What color is the ring around the edge of the Esso sign?

Hard questions (5 points):

12) A black rolling mechanic's board can be seen under one car. Which car?

13) How many identical lit lanterns are visible along the back wall?

14) Of the three stands in front of the cars, which has a three-pointed base?

15) On the third section of the wall from the left are hanging a number of window frames—enclosed shapes through which the wall is visible. How many of those can be seen in their entirety?

Your score: _____
Maximum base score: 41
Answers, page 173

Easy questions (1 point):

1) True or false: A game spinner is visible in the background.

2) Are any of the dominoes resting on one another?

3) Are any of the plastic, bowling pin–shaped playing pieces yellow?

4) Do the dominoes have square or rounded corners?

Medium questions (3 points):

5) How many white chessmen can be seen in the photo?

6) Which one of these colors of pick-up sticks does not appear at least once in the scene?
   a) yellow
   b) red
   c) black
   d) white

7) One domino sits in the center of the chessboard, surrounded by other game pieces. What two numbers are represented on the halves of that domino?

8) Near the bottom right of the scene are four pick-up sticks alongside one another. Three are the same color. Which is the most accurate description, from top to bottom?
   a) green, green, blue, green
   b) blue, green, blue, blue
   c) green, blue, green, green
   d) blue, blue, green, blue

9) There are two dice resting together on the chessboard. What two numbers do they show on their tops?

Hard questions (5 points):

10) There is only one playing piece standing upright in the photo. What color is it?

11) What lowercase letter on the border of the chessboard is partially covered by a domino with a single pip?

12) In the background is a die with six pips facing the camera. What color are the pips?

Your score: _____
Maximum base score: 34
Answers, page 173

Easy questions (1 point):

1) What is the name of the museum in the photo?

2) True or false: There is a person waving from the window over the clock in the float's tower.

3) Which of the three main clocks facing forward is highest—left, middle, or right?

4) What takes the place of the numbers on the clocks?

Medium questions (3 points):

5) How many lanes are visible on either side of the yellow line in the street?

6) What color are the flowers that ring the front of the parade float, on the right?

7) How many people are seated on the near side of the parade float?
   a) 10
   b) 14
   c) 16

8) Of the three main clocks facing forward, which is the only one whose face does not have an inner ring?

9) In Spanish and English, what word appears against a yellow-green background on two placards on the parade float?

10) How many leaves are on the giant rose display hanging on the museum?

Hard questions (5 points):

11) A white sign attached to the left end of the fence has a red number on it. What number is it?

12) Place these things in order from left to right in the picture: broken-off treetop, gray dome on roof of museum, man standing on roof of museum, Rose Parade banner hanging from lamppost, shadow of lamppost on wall of museum.

13) At the bottom of the picture, a number of people in the crowd are wearing the same cap, which has red and white stripes. What is notable about the one visible in the break in the fence?

14) What large image can be seen on the copper-green roof of the clock tower?

Your score: _____
Maximum base score: 42
Answers, page 173

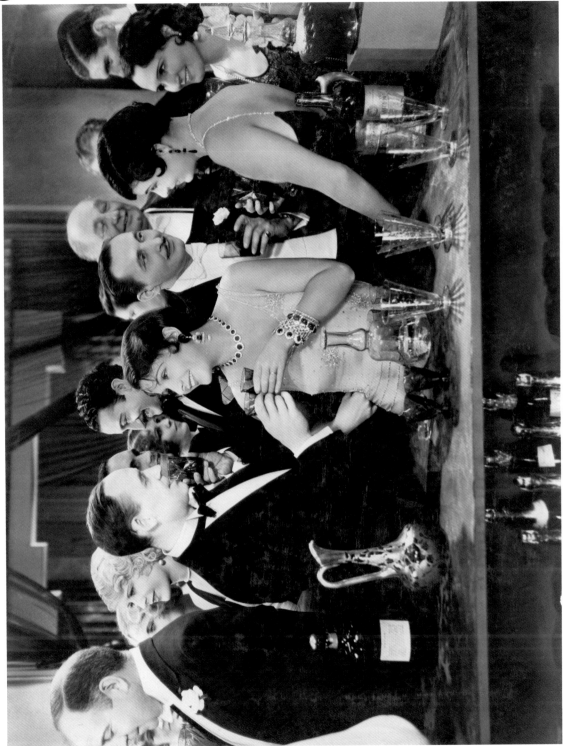

Easy questions (1 point):

1) Is the tall man at the far left wearing a boutonniere?

2) True or false: The glasses held by the couple in the center are touching.

3) Is anyone facing completely away from the camera?

4) Is the woman at the center of the picture holding her glass in her left or her right hand?

5) There is a liquor bottle on the left side of the bar. Does it show a label?

Medium questions (3 points):

6) Which one of the following is seen in the background of this scene?
   a) mirrors
   b) curtains
   c) paintings
   d) streamers and balloons
   e) a window with a city skyline

7) How many mustached men can be seen in the photo?

Hard questions (5 points):

8) Below the bar we can see the top of a number of champagne bottles. How many are there?
   a) 7
   b) 10
   c) 12

9) On which finger, if any, is the man to the right of the center couple wearing a ring?

10) There is a glass decanter on a raised platform on the far right of the photograph. What is the shape of the top of the decanter's stopper?
    a) round
    b) square
    c) pointed

11) Of the four women seen to be wearing earrings, how many of them are wearing dangling earrings as opposed to just studs?

Your score: _____
Maximum base score: 31
Answers, page 173

Easy questions (1 point):

1) True or false: The child's hand is painting a green egg.

2) Is the woman wearing a bracelet?

3) Do the planks on the wooden table run vertically or horizontally?

4) There are two plant pots in the photo: one at upper left, the other at lower right. One is yellow and the other is pale green. Which one is which?

5) True or false: The egg carton is holding ten eggs.

Medium questions (3 points):

6) How many paintbrushes are resting on the table?

7) What shape is the basket?
   a) rectangular
   b) oval
   c) circular

8) What is the main color of the paintbrush handle being held by the child?

9) Regarding the plaster bunny on the table, how many of its paws are visible from this overhead angle?

10) One of the table's planks has a prominent, egg-shaped knot. Which of these things is it closest to?
   a) the child's hand
   b) the woman's hand
   c) the plaster bunny
   d) the egg carton
   e) the fuzzy ears

Hard questions (5 points):

11) Which one of these describes an egg that does not appear in the scene?
   a) green with white polka dots
   b) blue with white stripes
   c) green with yellow and white stripes
   d) blue with red polka dots
   e) yellow with orange daisies

12) One of the triangular shapes on the left sports a zigzag pattern. Which two colors does it use?

13) Of the open jars of paint, which color is not there?
   a) yellow
   b) blue
   c) green
   d) white

Your score: _____
Maximum base score: 35
Answers, page 174

Easy questions (1 point):

1) True or false: There is one porthole visible on the green side of the boat.

2) Do any of the awnings in the background have stripes?

3) Are there any trees or greenery visible in the scene?

4) There is a woman with a two-toned blue jacket in the scene. Is she walking toward or away from the boat?

5) Do any of the roofs have a skylight visible?

Medium questions (3 points):

6) What item is hanging near the top of the boat's mast? For 3 extra points, what color is it?

7) What building material was used for the building at the far right of the scene, with the double chimney?

8) How many second-story windows are visible on the structure with the red window frames?

9) What is hanging near the top of the fence at the far left of the photograph?

Hard questions (5 points):

10) There is a ladder with a curved railing hanging off the pier and extending into the water. How many of its rungs are visible below the edge of the pier?

11) A gold sailboat emblem can be seen at the peak of a building near the middle of the scene. What shape immediately surrounds that sailboat?

12) On the two green pennants decorated with flowers, what are the colors of the flowers, from left to right?

Your score: _____
Maximum base score: 35
Answers, page 174

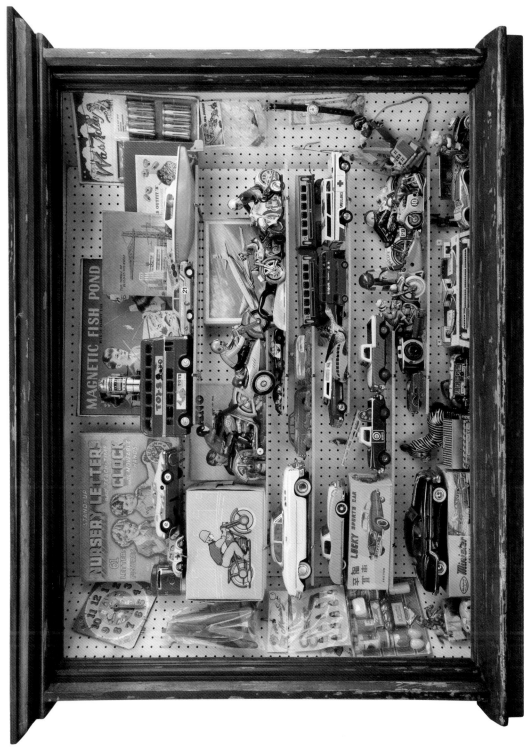

Easy questions (1 point):

1) Which way does the toy zebra face, right or left?

2) Is the motorcycle depicted on the large gray box a tandem-style or for a single passenger?

3) Which is on a lower shelf, the ambulance or the camera?

4) On the blue wood that frames the toy display, which part has lost more paint, the top or the bottom?

5) On the box showing the "Minister Delux" car, is the car depicted by itself or in a scene?

6) Is the backing of the toy clock round or square?

Medium questions (3 points):

7) There is a truck with a ladder. What color is the ladder? For 1 bonus point each, what two colors are the body of the truck?

8) What is the title on the display of toy clothespins?

9) How many Chinese characters are shown on the corner of the "Lucky Sports Car" box?

10) What word is advertised on the side of the large double-decker bus on the top shelf?

11) What title is on the game at top center?
    a) Magnetic Fish Game
    b) Magnetic Fish Fun
    c) Magnetic Fish Pond

12) What number is in the circle on the yellow racing car?

Hard questions (5 points):

13) What is in the white framed picture that shows a form of transportation?

14) What is hanging in front of the toy money and coins?

15) Place these items in order from top to bottom in the picture: fake fingernails, iron, pair of eggs, silver robot. For 3 bonus points, which of those four items is at approximately the same vertical position in the photo as the blue mechanical bird?

Your score: _____
Maximum base score: 44
Answers, page 174

Easy questions (1 point):

1) Are any books visible in the photograph?

2) Does the standing girl have her thumbs inside or outside her pockets?

3) Is the teacher wearing a watch?

4) There is a boy on the right with a striped shirt. Is the shirt long-sleeved or short-sleeved?

5) To the right is a cabinet with two doors side by side. Which one of the doors contains the keyhole?

6) Can we see either shoulder strap on the overalls of the standing girl?

Medium questions (3 points):

7) How many kids are sitting on the floor?

8) What is written in green letters at the top of the sign on the leftmost cabinet?
   a) Sound it out!
   b) Read to someone
   c) Make smart choices

9) What is notable about the girl sitting on the left side of the photograph?

10) How many strips of paper are pasted on the purple card on the whiteboard?

11) What kind of colorful design runs along the top of the five "class rules" sheets taped to the cabinet at right?
   a) balloons
   b) cars
   c) pennants
   d) stars

Hard questions (5 points):

12) In the numbered list of words on the whiteboard, what is the only five-letter word? For 3 bonus points, what is the only three-letter word?

13) Which way is this sign written?
   a) Class Rules
   b) Class rules
   c) Class rules:
   d) class rules:
   e) CLASS RULES

14) Of the five class rules, which two start with the same word?

Your score: _____
Maximum base score: 39
Answers, page 174

Easy questions (1 point):

1) Do the paper plates have a printed pattern?

2) True or false: The curtains in the background have tassels.

3) How many tines are on the plastic forks: three or four?

4) Two carving utensils with ornate blades are sitting next to each other on the table. Are they between the fruit-topped cake and the cheese plate, or between the cheese plate and the bowl of fruit?

5) Are any of the flower petals touching any of the food in the scene?

Medium questions (3 points):

6) As it is positioned on the cheese plate, is the top of the wedge of Swiss cheese square, rectangular, or tapered?

7) Name either of the two items between the stack of plates and the rear left corner of the table. For 2 bonus points, name both.

8) Approximately how many cupcakes are on the higher of the two plates?
   a) approximately 9
   b) approximately 13
   c) approximately 16

9) The decorated cake under the cupcakes is encircled by a ribbon of frosting. What color is the frosting?

Hard questions (5 points):

10) How many coffee cups are visible in the scene?

11) Which is the best description of the plastic utensils in the scene?
    a) pink plastic forks and knives
    b) red plastic forks
    c) red plastic forks and spoons
    d) purple plastic forks
    e) purple plastic forks and knives

12) What kind of fruit is on the far right side in the bowl of fruit?

13) How many flowers in the pot at the right are hanging downward?

14) What beige item is visible behind the plastic utensils?

Your score: _____
Maximum base score: 44
Answers, page 174

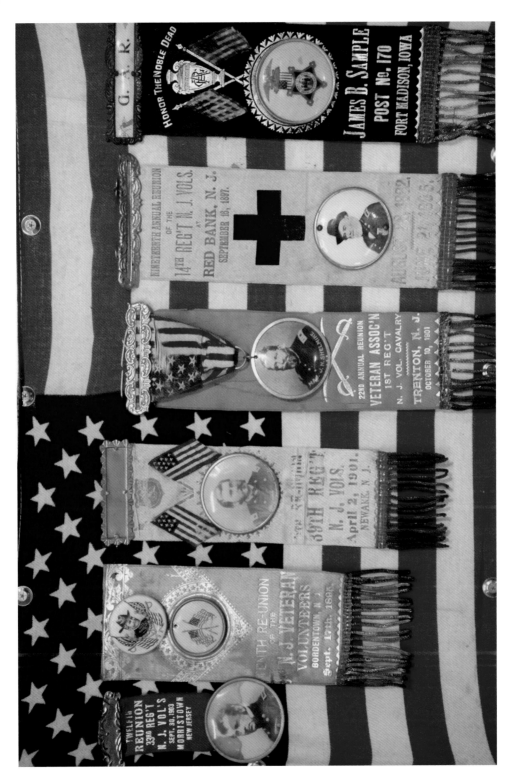

Easy questions (1 point):

1) True or false: Every man shown is clean-shaven.

2) Which is higher, the crossed swords on the yellow ribbon or the bottom edge of the field of blue on the background flag?

Medium questions (3 points):

3) How many of the ribbons have fringe?

4) What color are the tacks holding up the background flag?

5) All but one of the ribbons indicate regiments in New Jersey. What state is on the non–New Jersey ribbon?

6) Most of the ribbons have dates on them. What is the most recent year shown on a ribbon?

   a) 1897
   b) 1901
   c) 1903
   d) 1910

7) How many ribbons show pairs of flags?

8) Counting from the left, in what position is the smallest ribbon?

9) What color is the large cross on the Red Bank ribbon?

10) What initials appear at the top of the ribbon on the far right? (And for a bonus point, what letter is printed in red?)

11) How many of the ribbons are lacking a metal bar at the top?

Hard questions (5 points):

12) How many total times does the word "veteran" appear on the ribbons?

13) What rank is the officer pictured on the yellow ribbon?

14) In the circle in the ribbon on the far right there appears an insignia with a star shape. Does this star have five points, six, or eight?

Your score: _____
Maximum base score: 45
Answers, page 174

Easy questions (1 point):

1) True or false: The three dragon heads are all identically colored.

2) Can any trees be seen in the photograph?

3) Do the dragon heads show any teeth?

4) Are the canopies in the back pointed, or rounded like an umbrella?

Medium questions (3 points):

5) Counting from the bottom of the photograph, which boat's dragon head is not visible?

6) How many wave-like points can be seen on the rim of each boat near the dragon head?

7) What color are the scales of the front boat?
   a) blue, green, and cream
   b) brown, purple, and cream
   c) black, orange, and cream

8) What is the man standing in the rear boat holding?

9) How many people can be seen in the front boat?
   a) approximately 12
   b) approximately 16
   c) approximately 20

10) What color is the support below the fence in the background?

11) Counting from the bottom of the photograph, which boat's rowers have a series of white characters on the backs of their vests?

Hard questions (5 points):

12) Counting from the bottom of the photograph, which is the only boat to hold anyone wearing long sleeves?

13) In two of the boats, the rowers' hands are high, near the top of their stroke, and in two boats, the rowers' hands are low, near the bottom of their stroke. From the top down in the scene, what order is correct?
   a) high, high, low, low
   b) low, low, high, high
   c) high, low, high, low
   d) low, high, low, high

Your score: _____
Maximum base score: 35
Answers, page 174

Easy questions (1 point):

1) True or false: There is a white chair at the table in the foreground.

2) Is the shop's cash register visible in the photo?

3) On the top shelf there is a jar with a white lid. Next to it is a tin flowerpot with flowers in it. Which is taller, the white lid or the flowers?

4) Does the customer at the counter have his shirt tucked in?

5) Does the window on the left have curtains?

6) On the top shelf is a weathered portrait that is almost completely covered by something with a black-and-white zigzag pattern. Does that pattern run horizontally or vertically?

Medium questions (3 points):

7) Is the man behind the counter with his back to us wearing long sleeves, short sleeves, or rolled-up sleeves?

8) On the top shelf, there is a set of four solid-colored containers. Counting from the left, which of the four is the tallest? And for 3 bonus points, what color is it?

9) How is the woman grasping the coffee cup?
   a) by the middle
   b) by the handle
   c) by the bottom

10) On a shelf in the background is a stack of red napkins tied with a ribbon. What color is the ribbon?

Hard questions (5 points):

11) There are three kinds of baked goods on display on the counter: croissants, muffins, and scones. Place them in the correct order from left to right in the photo.

12) On the top shelf, on the left, there are a series of glasses with designs on them. Counting from left to right, which glass has a white cross on it?

13) On the top shelf, near the far right edge of the scene, are two bowls, one resting in the other. Which one of these is it?
   a) a red bowl resting inside a blue bowl
   b) a blue bowl resting inside a white bowl
   c) a blue bowl resting inside a red bowl

Your score: _____
Maximum base score: 36
Answers, page 174

Easy questions (1 point):

1) Is the green building near the left side of the photo a two-story or three-story building?

2) Are there any people in the scene?

3) Do any of the buildings' doorways have steps?

4) True or false: At least one of the TV antennas is a satellite dish.

5) Are any buildings painted a completely different color on the ground floor than they are above?

Medium questions (3 points):

6) What is the main color of the boat closest to the camera?

7) What two letters appear on the yellow sign at the far left of the photograph?

8) The roof area of one of the buildings is halfway through being painted. What color is being applied to the existing white wall?

9) How many panels are in each column of the door of the building closest to the camera?

10) What is the main color of the tall chimney that juts out above the skyline in the middle of the photo?

Hard questions (5 points):

11) What are the first five colors of the buildings here, starting from the left? (Ignore any white.)
    a) yellow, blue, green, gold, blue
    b) yellow, green, blue, gold, pink
    c) yellow, green, pink, gold, blue
    d) yellow, green, blue, gold, blue
    e) yellow, green, blue, pink, gold

12) What color is the building with the long billowing striped curtain hanging in front of its doorway?

13) Two of the first five buildings (starting from the left) have laundry hanging out to dry. Which two?

Your score: _____
Maximum base score: 35
Answers, page 174

144

Easy questions (1 point):

1) True or false: The seated guitar player is resting one of his arms on the top of the bar.

2) There are four coffee cups in a row on the second shelf. Are their handles facing left or right?

3) Is the doorway at the left covered with a door or a curtain?

4) True or false: Of the two belt buckles visible, one is rectangular and the other is oval.

Medium questions (3 points):

5) How many men have their pants cuffs rolled up?

6) Which one of these items is the only one NOT seen along the back wall?
   a) a light switch
   b) a fly swatter
   c) a rolling pin
   d) a jug

7) What instrument is being played by the man wearing the black hat?

8) How many of the men have bandannas tied around their necks?

9) What are the initials of the name that appears on the guitar of the guitar player seated at the bar?
   a) J.W.
   b) J.K.
   c) M.W.
   d) M.K.

10) How many coffee cups can be seen, in total, hanging from hooks under the first shelf?
   a) 6
   b) 8
   c) 10

Hard questions (5 points):

11) What kind of symbol appears near the sound hole on the fretboard of the guitar on the right?

12) How many buttons are on the visible shirt cuff of the man playing the bass?

Your score: _____
Maximum base score: 32
Answers, page 175

Easy questions (1 point):

1) True or false: The rocking horse has a padded seat.

2) Do the Christmas decorations along the mantelpiece drape over its side edges?

3) Is there any snow in the scene?

4) True or false: There is a star at the top of the tree.

5) Does the clock on the mantelpiece have a visible pendulum?

Medium questions (3 points):

6) How many curlicues, suggesting the curls of a powdered wig, are on each side of the Nutcracker's head?

7) What are the walls of the room made of?

8) What color are the rocking horses on the tree?

9) How many stockings are hanging on the fireplace?

10) What color are the Nutcracker's eyes?

11) In front of the fireplace, there is a gift on the floor wrapped with red paper. How many candles are around it?

Hard questions (5 points):

12) How many panes of glass are on the door on the right?
   a) 20 (five rows by four columns)
   b) 30 (six rows by five columns)
   c) 35 (seven rows by five columns)
   d) 42 (seven rows by six columns)

13) There is a cylindrical gift on the floor. Which description of that gift is most accurate?
   a) gold paper, red ribbon, bow
   b) gold paper, red ribbon, no bow
   c) red paper, gold ribbon, bow
   d) red paper, gold ribbon, no bow

Your score: _____
Maximum base score: 33
Answers, page 175

Easy questions (1 point):

1) Are all the U.S. flags the same size?

2) True or false: Appropriately, the elephants and the donkeys face in opposite directions.

3) Which color is higher on all of the looped awareness-style ribbons, red or blue?

Medium questions (3 points):

4) How many stars appear on the Capitol building icon?

5) Which one of these things does not appear as an icon?

   a) star
   b) prize ribbon
   c) Uncle Sam
   d) voting checkbox

6) What icon represents the southernmost point of Texas?

7) Several icons appear in both red-only and blue-only versions. For which one of these is that not the case?

   a) envelope
   b) megaphone
   c) thumbs up
   d) thumbs down

8) How many kinds of living creatures appear as icons?

Hard questions (5 points):

9) The word VOTE (with a checkmark representing the V) appears four times in the map. What is notable about the placement of all four VOTE icons?

10) Which icon appears the fewest number of times? For 5 bonus points, how many times does it appear?

11) What large icon constitutes most of Michigan's Lower Peninsula, the "mitten"?

12) How many envelopes make up part of the West Coast, where it borders the Pacific Ocean?

Your score: _____
Maximum base score: 43
Answers, page 175

Easy questions (1 point):

1) Does any book cover show a person?

2) True or false: The book *Room*, on the middle shelf with a white spine, is shown in two different sizes.

3) Which red book appears further to the left, *The Skin Collector* or *The Red Tent?*

Medium questions (3 points):

4) What type of animal appears in yellow on the cover of *The Enchanted?*

5) Who is the main author of *Havana Storm*, whose cover shows a burning vessel on the water?

6) How many books are shown face-forward?
   a) 4
   b) 7
   c) 9

7) One book appears face-forward with two different cover designs. What is its title?

8) What is the largest word on the round sticker on the cover of the centrally placed *All the Light We Cannot See?*

9) How many copies of Roald Dahl's book, which has a white spine with a little bit of pink on it, appear on the top shelf?

10) One book's cover looks like a vinyl record. What is the book's title?

Hard questions (5 points):

11) A stack of books with the names Del Toro and Hogan appear on the top shelf at the right, titled (in red) *The Fall, The Strain*, and *The Night Eternal*. Which of those titles appears at the far left of the middle shelf?

12) How many Jeffery Deaver books can be seen in the photograph? (Count each copy as a separate book.)

13) A book on the bottom shelf has its title appearing in four shapes on its spine. What kind of shapes are they?
   a) squares
   b) circles
   c) triangles
   d) hexagons

14) The books are alphabetized by author, but the F section at the lower right isn't in correct order. What is the last name of the author whose books incorrectly separate the books by Joy Fielding and Helen Fielding?

Your score: _____
Maximum base score: 44
Answers, page 175

Easy questions (1 point):

1) True or false: Every clock is either round, square, or octagonal.

2) Is the clock with the blue face cut off, or shown in full?

3) There is an octagonal clock near the bottom center that reads about 5:00. Does it have a second hand?

Medium questions (3 points):

4) How many clocks can be seen in their entirety?

5) What does it say on the round clock with the red face?

6) There are two almost identical clocks in the cut-off rows at the top and bottom. What is the main color of their borders?

7) What shape is the smallest clock?

8) Where is the clock that reads 3:30:20?
   a) at the far right near the center of the column
   b) at the upper left
   c) third in the row closest to the bottom that can be seen in its entirety

9) Of the clocks that can be seen in their entirety, how many have no numerals, Roman or Arabic?

Hard questions (5 points):

10) On the rightmost clock with Roman numerals, between what two numbers is the minute hand? And for a bonus point, is the number 4 represented on that clock as IIII or IV?

11) What is the color of the numbers of the uppermost clock that can be seen in its entirety in the rightmost column?

12) Put these clocks in order from left to right:
    A: Square clock with red face
    B: Round clock with dark blue border
    C: Octagonal clock with a gold frame
    D: Round clock with light green border
    a) B, D, C, A
    b) C, D, A, B
    c) B, D, A, C
    d) C, B, D, A

13) One clock registers the day and date in a spot on its face. Where on its face does this appear?

Your score: _____
Maximum base score: 42
Answers, page 175

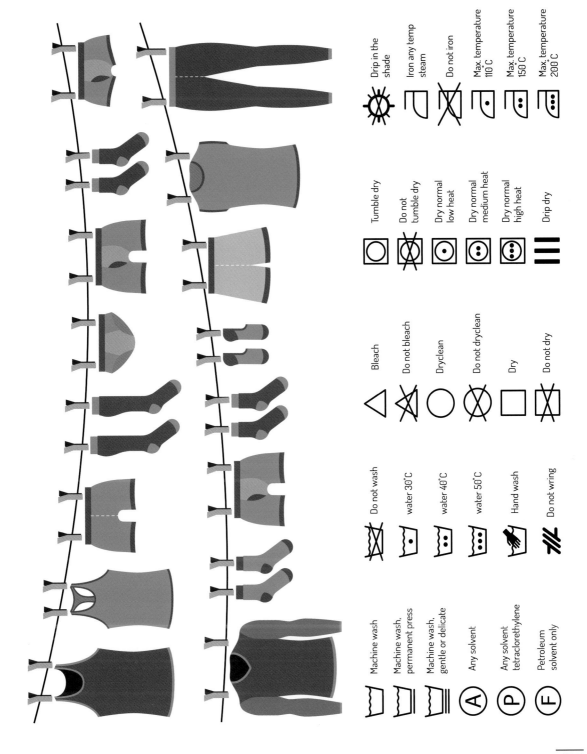

Drip in the shade

Iron any temp steam

Do not iron

Max. temperature 110° C

Max. temperature 150° C

Max. temperature 200° C

Tumble dry

Do not tumble dry

Dry normal low heat

Dry normal medium heat

Dry normal high heat

Drip dry

Bleach

Do not bleach

Dryclean

Do not dryclean

Dry

Do not dry

Do not wash

water 30°C

water 40°C

water 50°C

Hand wash

Do not wring

Machine wash

Machine wash, permanent press

Machine wash, gentle or delicate

Any solvent

Any solvent tetraclorethylene

Petroleum solvent only

155

Easy questions (1 point):

1) True or false: None of the clothespins actually touch the clothes.

2) Are temperatures indicated in Fahrenheit or Celsius?

3) Which appears higher in the icons, the sun or the hand?

4) Are all of the pairs of underwear different?

Medium questions (3 points):

5) How many rows and columns of icons are there?
a) 5 columns, 5 rows
b) 5 columns, 6 rows
c) 6 columns, 5 rows
d) 6 columns, 6 rows

6) What does an increasing number of dots indicate in the icons?

7) What is the main color of the long-sleeved shirt?

8) How many icons include a large X?
a) 3
b) 5
c) 7

9) Counting from left to right, which column of icons appears directly under the leggings?

10) What is the correct order of these icons, from left to right?
a) Any solvent, Hand wash, Tumble dry
b) Any solvent, Tumble dry, Hand wash
c) Hand wash, Any solvent, Tumble dry
d) Hand wash, Tumble dry, Any solvent
e) Tumble dry, Any solvent, Hand wash
f) Tumble dry, Hand wash, Any solvent

11) How many clothespins are there?
a) 20
b) 26
c) 32

Hard questions (5 points):

12) What does a triangle icon indicate?

13) What is the symbol for drip dry?

Your score: _____
Maximum base score: 35
Answers, page 175

Easy questions (1 point):

1) True or false: The prizes include SpongeBob SquarePants.

2) What color is the padding on the countertop in front of the seats?

3) How many numbered stations are there?

4) The carnival stools alternate between purple and green. What color stool is first, at the far left?

Medium questions (3 points):

5) Which kind of animal is not represented as a stuffed toy prize?
   a) elephant
   b) pig
   c) cow

6) What is notable about the pile of prizes just behind the counter, on the far left?

7) How many thin, dark stripes are there around the edge of each seat?

8) What prize is resting on the counter?

9) On the rainbow-striped teddy bears, the bottoms of the bears' feet are what color?

10) What word can be read on the sign just below the giant banana prizes?

Hard questions (5 points):

11) In the game, the target is a hole in the center of a flowery burst of colors. What color is the outline of the centermost part of this target?

12) A carnival worker can be seen restocking the prizes while standing on part of the game platform. What number is he standing in front of?

13) Of the giant banana prizes hanging high over the seats in the middle of the photo, approximately how many of their smiles are visible?
   a) approximately 5
   b) approximately 9
   c) approximately 13

14) What two color choices are there for the bunny head with the bow tie?

Your score: _____
Maximum base score: 42
Answers, page 175

6 min.

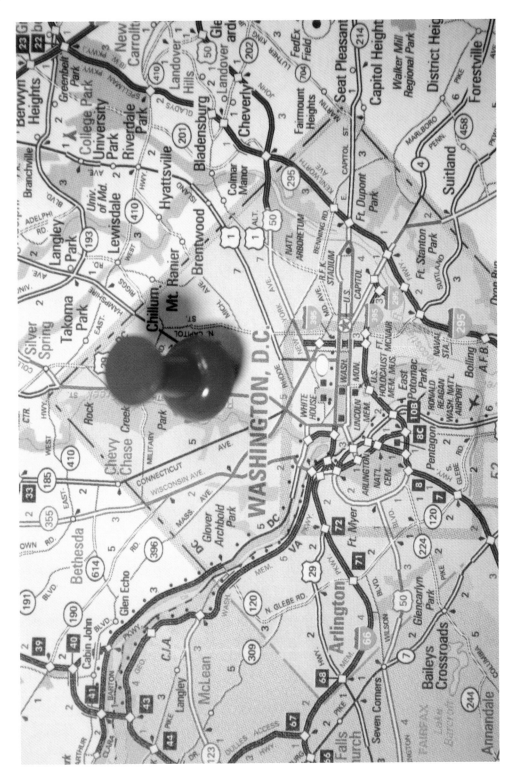

Easy questions (1 point):

1) True or false: The dashed lines marking the diamond-shaped border of Washington, D.C., are all the same length.

2) Is the town near the southwest corner of the map punctuated as Bailey's Crossroads or Baileys Crossroads?

3) Does the White House fall north or south of the red thumbtack?

Medium questions (3 points):

4) What special symbol is used to denote the U.S. Capitol?

5) Which is the correct order of these locations from west to east, all shown in red type?
   a) Landover Hills, McLean, Silver Spring
   b) Landover Hills, Silver Spring, McLean
   c) McLean, Landover Hills, Silver Spring
   d) McLean, Silver Spring, Landover Hills
   e) Silver Spring, Landover Hills, McLean
   f) Silver Spring, McLean, Landover Hills

6) There are three interstate highway numbers shown on the map, with their distinctive red, white, and blue logos. Take 3 points for each number you can name.

7) What color is used to show the paths of the interstate highways?

8) What is the name of the thoroughfare partially obscured by the red thumbtack on the thumbtack's east?
   a) N. Capitol St.
   b) New York Ave.
   c) Rock Creek Rd.

9) What is the largest, boldest name on the map besides Washington, D.C.?

Hard questions (5 points):

10) Highway exit numbers appear in white inside small black boxes. Two such numbers appear in the northeast corner, far from any others. What are they?
    a) 7 and 8
    b) 22 and 23
    c) 40 and 41
    d) 67 and 68

11) What black symbol appears at the bottom center of the map, just to the west of the water there?

12) Which best describes the type style of the landmarks on the map, such as the White House?
    a) black, initial capital letters, not italicized
    b) black, full capital letters, italicized
    c) red, initial capital letters, not italicized
    d) red, full capital letters, italicized

Your score: _____
Maximum base score: 42
Answers, page 175

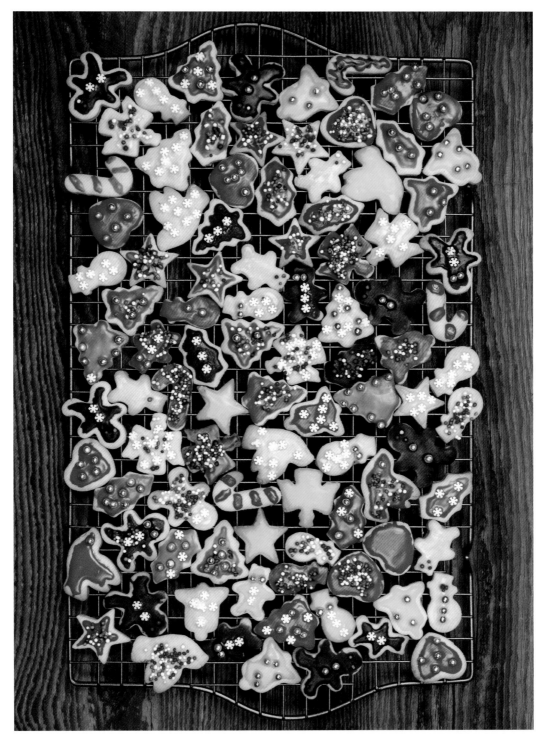

Easy questions (1 point):

1) True or false: The cookie in the lower left corner of the cooling rack is a gingerbread man with brown frosting.

2) Does the wood grain in the background run horizontally or vertically?

3) Which are there more of, plain, cookie-colored doves or plain, cookie-colored snowmen?

4) Are there any brown sprinkles on the cookies?

Medium questions (3 points):

5) Which one of these shapes does not appear?
a) angel
b) sleigh
c) holly leaf
d) bell

6) There are five candy cane cookies. How many of them are decorated just with red stripes?

7) Which best describes the edges of the cooling rack?
a) they are all straight
b) the left and right edges have semicircular projections directly across from each other
c) the left and right edges have semicircular projections not directly across from each other

8) What shape are the sprinkles that aren't round?

9) How many of the cookies are frosted yellow?
a) 5
b) 8
c) 11

Hard questions (5 points):

10) All of the hearts are red except one. How is it frosted differently from the others? For 5 extra points, where is it on the rack?

11) Imagine the cooling rack is divided into four quadrants. Which quadrant contains no yellow-frosted cookies?

12) In the approximate center of the rack are two Christmas tree-shaped cookies, one green and one red. What is the shape and color of the cookie between them? (Give yourself 3 points if you get the shape or color correct, but not both.)

13) How many cookies are shown?
a) 50
b) 65
c) 80
d) 95

Your score: _____
Maximum base score: 44
Answers, page 176

6 min.

Easy questions (1 point):

1) Which red-and-white cards are higher, Burlington or T.J. Maxx?

2) Can you buy a card for gas here?

Medium questions (3 points):

3) Which merchant commands the most spots? For 3 extra points, how many spots?

4) What shape is formed by the French fries on the McDonald's cards?

5) Only one of the detachable plastic cards is dark purple, shown on a black background. Which one is it?

   a) Forever 21
   b) Express
   c) Lane Bryant
   d) DSW

6) How many styles of Barnes & Noble cards are there?

7) Give yourself 3 points for naming each of the two Disney characters shown.

8) What location is given in the Aeropostale logo?

9) How many columns of gift cards are shown?

   a) 10
   b) 12
   c) 14

10) Which one of these is true of iTunes and Google Play cards?

    a) both are in the photo
    b) only iTunes is in the photo
    c) only Google Play is in the photo
    d) neither is in the photo

Hard questions (5 points):

11) What two colors appear on the Nike card?

12) What is unusual about the two Nordstrom cards?

13) If you want a $25 Bass Pro Shops card, which color should you buy?

14) What phrase is printed on the Chili's gift card (which displays a red chili pepper)?

Your score: _____
Maximum base score: 52
Answers, page 176

Easy questions (1 point):

1) Two identical butterflies appear side by side at the very bottom. Are they in the right half or the left half of the picture?

2) There are three butterflies with purple-blue wings on the top and brown wings on the bottom. Are they the same size as each other?

Medium questions (3 points):

3) The butterflies along the left side line up roughly in a column. How many butterflies make up that column?

4) What are the two main colors of the largest butterfly?

5) How many butterflies are in the picture?
   a) 45
   b) 58
   c) 70
   d) 82

6) Which of these color combinations does not appear on any butterfly?
   a) white and brown
   b) green and purple
   c) brown and yellow
   d) blue and black

7) An orange, black, and white monarch-style butterfly appears at the top right corner. How many total butterflies with that design are shown?

Hard questions (5 points):

8) What are the three main colors of the butterfly at the lower left?

9) There are two matching mostly white butterflies in the picture, with a little light orange and gray. Where are they?
   a) on the far left and far right
   b) on the top and the bottom
   c) both near the center
   d) one on the left and one on the bottom

10) There is one butterfly whose design does not match that of at least one other butterfly shown. In what quadrant of the picture does it appear: upper left, upper right, lower left, or lower right?

Your score: _____
Maximum base score: 32
Answers, page 176

PAGES 7-8

1) a) red for men, blue for women
2) Yes, a nurse's cap
3) b) a short-sleeved shirt
4) No
5) Electropathic & Zander Institute
6) Three
7) c) proven
8) 52
9) Four
10) a) Pamphlets and Consultations
11) The Medical Battery Co. Ltd.
12) Debility and hysteria
13) b) Mr. C.B. Harness
14) Physic

PAGES 9-10

1) False
2) a) the girl on the left
3) No
4) The string over her left shoulder
5) Yes
6) It's a right hand
7) c) a stuffed pelican and a stuffed alligator
8) Her ears
9) a) wooden planks
10) 9
11) b) it is held back by a hairband and is in a bun
12) a) approximately 8
13) Hands

PAGES 11-12

1) False
2) It's standing on its lid
3) Yes
4) Yes
5) 21
6) Four
7) Gold
8) a) wooden zigzags
9) 1903
10) White
11) c) non-concentric circles divided by two straight vertical lines
12) Three
13) a) on the far right and far left of the picture
14) A speaker
15) Yellow (or tan/beige); diamond

PAGES 13-14

1) True
2) a) tapering points
3) Over
4) a) yes
5) Four
6) c) a rubber band
7) Black (count dark blue as correct)
8) A cross
9) a) none
10) b) wings
11) The strap end is lower than the watch
12) b) white
13) One, on his left thumb

PAGES 15-16

1) False
2) Left
3) No
4) 1776
5) b) 8
6) c) alternating gold triangles and gray lines
7) Nine
8) Red
9) b) SEAL
10) Three
11) c) there is one inside the words and two outside them
12) There is no dot there, as there is between all the other words

PAGES 17-18

1) Right
2) False
3) Open (there are many more)
4) Yes
5) Vertically
6) Three
7) b) green and white stripes
8) Eight
9) Green
10) Marshmallows
11) Four
12) Yellow

PAGES 19-20

1) A left hand
2) True
3) Yes (one, in the tip at far left)
4) Just on the top
5) Pink
6) c) 10
7) Neither
8) Green
9) Four
10) b) How to make a selfie
11) Three
12) b) 4
13) Remote Viewfinder

PAGES 21-22

1) False (the man at the far left is wearing glasses)
2) Right
3) Yes
4) The tips of the roof's corners
5) Yes
6) c) 8
7) A bird
8) a) collections of large stones
9) Black and red
10) Five
11) c) they appear right side up and upside down
12) The first one

PAGES 23-24

1) False
2) The one for "Stagecoach"
3) No, they don't go all the way to the right
4) Four
5) c) "The Wizard of Oz"
6) The Eiffel Tower
7) Mate (from "Tarzan and His Mate")
8) a) Db 1000
9) One
10) Horse
11) James Cagney
12) Five
13) "Gone With the Wind"
14) 1995/B
15) Two

PAGES 25-26
1) True
2) 10 of diamonds
3) No
4) Four levels; three floor levels
5) Blue and white
6) Diamonds
7) c) in all four corners
8) Hearts
9) b) one is visible on each card
10) 5
11) Five
12) d) rectangular with rounded corners
13) The third level down
14) Zero

PAGES 27-28
1) Yellow
2) True
3) No
4) The hands of the man kneeling at the right
5) Two
6) b) Grace Dorgan Porter
7) Green and blue
8) c) It extends through all three main panels and is partially hidden by a piece of fabric in one panel and a garland of flowers in another
9) Two
10) Red
11) Six
12) Flowers
13) Seven

PAGES 29-30
1) No
2) False
3) Serif
4) Yes
5) Loop tail
6) Innovation (the only red word)
7) b) orange
8) Process, product, business
9) d) technology
10) c) proper nouns (Oslo, Europe, etc.) and f) initialisms (GNP)
11) Learning
12) c) users

PAGES 31-32
1) A double door
2) False
3) The blue door with the double-arched yellow frame
4) Eight
5) c) a tree with curved branches
6) Etc.; three times
7) b) brown wood
8) a) 1
9) second from the bottom
10) c) 2

PAGES 33-34
1) The woman
2) The right side
3) The top circle is connected
4) Brown
5) a) drink more water
6) e) black, green, blue
7) c) lungs
8) Gray
9) a) one up, one down
10) Four
11) b) Health & Medical
12) Zero

PAGES 35-36
1) The bill with the waving man
2) Yes (at the bottom left, below the U.S. dollar)
3) Our right
4) Three; $1, $10, $20
5) c) Tanzania
6) b) 2
7) a) 6
8) b) kwacha
9) 500
10) c) both the number 1000 and the word MILLE

PAGES 37-38
1) No
2) The small group of large ones
3) No
4) At the same angle
5) Yes
6) The limes
7) c) lower left
8) Two
9) d) over 15, attached together by their greenery in two batches
10) Four
11) b) a pumpkin
12) a) trio of red apples, trio of green apples, pair of yellow pears, broccoli

PAGES 39-40
1) Right
2) No
3) Flowers (daisies)
4) On the dark green backing
5) From upper left to lower right
6) No
7) Three (two appearing partially at the top left, and the large one on the right)
8) Black
9) The numbers run counterclockwise
10) Piano keys
11) a) dots on the inside ring; Roman numerals on the outside ring
12) Dark red/maroon
13) A metal disk (probably a pendulum)
14) Three

PAGES 41-42
1) No
2) Necktie
3) a) like this: I
4) On the other side
5) 8
6) b) approximately 10
7) A bell
8) b) Proverbs And Sayings
9) art; salary
10) All work and no play makes Jack a dull boy (the words "Jack a" are obscured by the teacher's head)
11) prescrible

PAGES 43-44
1) Yes, in two parts of the photo
2) Yes
3) False
4) No
5) Five
6) Dark blue and white
7) a) none
8) Aldwych Theatre
9) Just b) dirt
10) Four
11) Orange
12) Six

PAGES 45-46
1) False
2) No
3) Vertically
4) Left
5) No
6) c) a little blue sky on the left, gray clouds on the right
7) A barrel
8) The folding chair
9) It has a period at the end
10) a) desert landscape, cactus, low mountains in the distance
11) d) 1920
12) None
13) 14

PAGES 47-48
1) Blue with a white stripe
2) The ground
3) a) red
4) No
5) b) from right to left
6) Nurse
7) b) four or five
8) A period
9) b) marvelous
10) A fired cannon
11) Six
12) A bayonet

PAGES 49-50
1) False
2) Yes
3) It's the other way around
4) Toward the camera
5) False
6) His left side
7) b) approximately 10
8) One
9) Yellow
10) d) 5
11) G

PAGES 51-52
1) The high neon sign
2) b) a mountain
3) Upside down
4) No
5) To the left
6) b) turquoise, purple, red, yellow
7) Eight
8) 11:50 (despite the sunset view)
9) Soda Fountain
10) None of them
11) Pink
12) Two
13) A jukebox

PAGES 53-54
1) False
2) Behind
3) No
4) His fingers
5) The hand holding the microphone
6) No
7) Two
8) The bottoms
9) Oriental rug
10) Green
11) Five
12) Three

PAGES 55-56
1) False
2) His right ear
3) More white chips
4) No
5) They stand up
6) Left
7) Two
8) The man in the middle
9) The man on the right
10) One
11) c) approximately 14
12) It's a clip-on tie with one of the clips showing
13) Three

PAGES 57-58
1) In front
2) On the top
3) Yes
4) True (it is pointing between the 46 and 47 second marks)
5) From upper left to lower right
6) IIII
7) Yes, on the left
8) It is red (the other numerals are black)
9) The watch's gears
10) b) round
11) White
12) One—the innermost ring
13) 13

PAGES 59-60

1) Yes
2) His left hand
3) True
4) Four
5) White
6) Two
7) Light blue
8) None
9) a) 54.49
10) Three
11) a) stripes
12) 0.05
13) He is using his left hand to hold the phone to his right ear

PAGES 61-62

1) c) The Rules for Good Teeth
2) No
3) False
4) Pointed top
5) The toothbrush
6) No
7) Four fingers and a thumb
8) No
9) b) can't look after themselves
10) Celery
11) Five
12) To wash away sticky foods
13) b) a dental mirror
14) Zero
15) a) sweet, sticky foods
16) Zero
17) His tie

PAGES 63-64

1) False
2) No
3) The one on the left
4) Long-sleeved
5) The top pieces are longer than the bottom ones
6) One
7) An umbrella
8) b) gravel
9) Two
10) Four
11) Behind his back
12) 5
13) Green

PAGES 65-66

1) False
2) The one on the left
3) Roman numerals
4) Yes (10 sections)
5) No
6) Black
7) b) approximately 9:29
8) Green and red
9) c) 20
10) It only has one hand
11) Six
12) c) 9

PAGES 67-68

1) False
2) On his left side
3) Yes
4) Square edges
5) They are inside
6) No
7) Light blue
8) b) an unbuttoned long-sleeved shirt over a T-shirt
9) Four
10) Knobs
11) a) side by side
12) A plant with flowers
13) c) the two outer flaps are visible but they are not sealed
14) Zigzags

PAGES 69-70

1) False
2) No
3) Her left
4) No
5) Three
6) Leaves
7) b) somewhat more than half
8) Five
9) Crisper
10) a) stars
11) A toaster
12) Eggs, Canada Dry bottle, Tip-Top bread, platter of dessert cups with whipped cream

PAGES 71-72

1) Horizontally
2) No
3) The right side
4) No
5) Smiling
6) No
7) a) 15
8) Dark wood
9) Jagged or zigzag
10) A leaf (and vines)
11) b) one (second from the left on the top)
12) It has green smudges
13) Three

PAGES 73-74

1) Closed
2) Yellow; two pairs
3) The right half
4) Yes
5) Six
6) Two
7) Red
8) b) rabbit
9) One (the tallest figure, whose leg coverings are rendered to look translucent)
10) The tail of the animal skin used to make the piece of clothing
11) Both
12) One
13) Two

PAGES 75-76

1) No
2) Four-door
3) Yes, at the left
4) Yes, the one at the left
5) 11:48
6) Three
7) Amtrak
8) c) 7P74
9) 32nd
10) Two
11) O
12) Weekdays 6:00-10:00 A.M.
13) Four

PAGES 77-78

1) Yellow and blue
2) a) one
3) No
4) Summer—they are green
5) Lower left to upper right
6) c) parallel with the railing
7) Two—the front two
8) a) sand
9) a) approximately 10
10) Purple and yellow
11) A basket
12) b) black leather straps with studs

PAGES 79-80

1) False
2) Right
3) Open
4) Yes
5) No
6) Right-handed
7) 3
8) a) sideburns
9) Round
10) One
11) It has no temples (sidepieces)
12) Two

PAGES 81-82

1) True
2) It is tucked into her waistband
3) A man (he has a beard)
4) Right
5) No
6) A closed one
7) B and P
8) DePaul
9) 21
10) A megaphone
11) c) an American flag
12) 44
13) V, D, V
14) Three

PAGES 83-84

1) They are on the same shelf
2) No
3) False
4) To the left
5) No
6) Yellow
7) Fire extinguishers
8) Four (three on the floor, one on a shelf)
9) Blue (with a white top)
10) It is not on the bicycle (it can be seen in the corner behind the flowerpots)
11) Gray and green
12) A cooler (it is in the corner near a red duffel bag)
13) A (gray) electrical box's cover

PAGES 85-86

1) True (Kellogg's)
2) No
3) Top row
4) Cocoa Krispies and Froot Loops
5) b) Gr-r-reat!
6) Crackle
7) Corn Flakes
8) Cocoa Krispies and Frosted Flakes
9) c) red, yellow, green
10) One (Pops)
11) Corn Flakes
12) b) Puffed
13) Leaves
14) a) blue and yellow
15) Cocoa Krispies
16) Pink

PAGES 87-88

1) Left
2) To the right
3) True
4) Exterior
5) Orange and yellow (give yourself credit for "red and yellow")
6) b) in the middle
7) Seven
8) Love
9) Pink
10) Horses
11) One
12) Red

PAGES 89-90

1) False
2) Sweatpants
3) The right leg
4) No
5) Yes
6) False
7) Blue
8) a) 7
9) Two
10) c) red, green, black
11) None
12) One (the woman on the left)

PAGES 91-92

1) False
2) No
3) No
4) Left
5) False
6) No
7) Red
8) b) Museu Picasso
9) Sneakers
10) Red
11) a) large paving stones and cobblestones
12) They are covered with metal cuffs

PAGES 93-94

1) Open
2) Yes
3) False
4) Away from
5) From upper right to lower left
6) b) a rectangular frame with an oval mat
7) Four
8) A top hat
9) b) oval
10) Three
11) A pin
12) One

PAGES 95-96

1) False
2) Yes (most prominently at the upper right)
3) Left
4) Closed
5) Right
6) Two
7) c) Games, Gifts & Souvenirs
8) Umbrellas
9) York
10) £6.99
11) c) 27 (nine columns by three rows)
12) Green
13) Three

PAGES 97-98

1) True
2) Blue
3) They go to the edges
4) No
5) Left
6) No
7) Black
8) a) at the top
9) Pencils; two
10) Blue
11) b) toward the rubber band ball
12) MU

PAGES 99-100

1) False
2) White
3) No
4) At her chest
5) No
6) No
7) b) one gold, one red
8) Down
9) Black
10) b) approximately 6
11) It is missing its black emblem
12) One
13) c) two to the right and one to the left

PAGES 101-102

1) False (the elephant only appears in the small game)
2) The sun
3) No (red and orange should be swapped, and violet is missing too)
4) Gold
5) An ace of diamonds
6) The highest is $50,000 and the lowest is $20
7) Cherries, strawberry, watermelon
8) Canada
9) Blue
10) c) elephant, ladybug, bird
11) 5
12) A club
13) Four
14) $100
15) a) swirly yellow and brown stripes

PAGES 103-104

1) False
2) No
3) No
4) Parallel
5) a) a plant
6) Red
7) c) the bottom
8) A candle
9) b) over the right side of the two-seater
10) A moose
11) They stop at the midpoint (they do not go all the way around)
12) Seven
13) Four

PAGES 105-106

1) False
2) No
3) Yes
4) No
5) a) black
6) c) VisitNebraska.com
7) CALGARY
8) d) solid-colored shirts, vests
9) Teal
10) d) cupping her face
11) Vertically on the blue railing

PAGES 107-108

1) True
2) Yes
3) The same person
4) A man
5) True
6) Right
7) Three
8) Beige/tan
9) Two
10) A handbag
11) Three
12) The first and second
13) Black (or dark gray)
14) Three
15) Her index finger is up along the edge

PAGES 109-110
1) False
2) Yes
3) Her right
4) Behind
5) No
6) One
7) a) approximately 12
8) At the top
9) Two
10) b) her index finger and pinkie
11) A piano
12) b) both far hands (those farthest from the camera)

PAGES 111-112
1) Toward
2) The cranberry sauce
3) The pepper
4) Right
5) Off
6) Yellow and orange
7) Biscuits
8) Three
9) Lemon slices
10) Square
11) Three
12) b) approximately 15
13) It has a handle

PAGES 113-114
1) The one on the left
2) No
3) a) approximately 4:00 (it's about 3:55)
4) True, to the left of the tallest spire
5) It's a painted platform
6) Right
7) a) and c)
8) White and blue
9) b) 8 (there is another row of pillars behind the front ones)
10) Yellow
11) Snowflakes
12) Green, white, and orange

PAGES 115-116
1) No
2) No
3) True
4) The angel's wings
5) No
6) Rounded
7) Yes (probably a violin)
8) Two
9) Red
10) A bow and arrow
11) b) approximately 15
12) Gold
13) They're dotted
14) Jewelry box, candle, mask, flowers

PAGES 117-118
1) Yes
2) Hoops
3) Men
4) a) "at" sign and star
5) Orange
6) Dark Ages
7) b) trees
8) Scientists
9) Green
10) b) Support
11) ff
12) SUPP

PAGES 119-120
1) No
2) False
3) Horizontally
4) Yes
5) The lighter shade
6) Left
7) Red
8) Four
9) c) DEALER
10) They are near each other at the center
11) Blue
12) The nearer blue car
13) Three
14) The middle one
15) Six

PAGES 121-122
1) False
2) No
3) Yes
4) Rounded
5) Seven
6) c) black
7) Six and four
8) c) green, blue, green, green
9) Three and six
10) Red
11) b
12) Blue

PAGES 123-124
1) Norton Simon Museum
2) False
3) Middle
4) Faces
5) Two on each side
6) Yellow
7) c) 16
8) The middle one
9) Vida and life
10) Three
11) 4
12) Banner, treetop, dome, man, shadow
13) It has a red pompom
14) A crescent man in the moon

PAGES 125-126
1) Yes
2) True
3) No
4) Her left hand
5) Yes
6) b) curtains
7) Two
8) a) 7
9) His pinkie
10) c) pointed
11) All four

PAGES 127-128
1) True
2) No
3) Vertically
4) Upper left is yellow, lower right is pale green
5) True
6) Two
7) b) oval
8) Purple
9) One
10) d) the egg carton
11) d) blue with red polka dots
12) Pink and white
13) c) green (despite the fact that the child is painting a green egg)

PAGES 129-130
1) False
2) Yes
3) No
4) Toward the boat
5) Yes (three of them do)
6) An orange bucket
7) Brick
8) Three
9) A life preserver
10) Four
11) A circle
12) Yellow, purple

PAGES 131-132
1) Left
2) Single passenger
3) The camera
4) The bottom
5) In a scene
6) Square (it has slightly rounded corners)
7) Yellow; blue and white
8) Washday
9) Four
10) Toys
11) c) Magnetic Fish Pond
12) 21
13) An airplane
14) A watch (at the right)
15) Robot, iron, fingernails, eggs; the fingernails

PAGES 133-134
1) No
2) Inside
3) No
4) Short-sleeved
5) The one on the right
6) No
7) Seven
8) b) Read to someone
9) She has a flower in her hair
10) Three
11) c) pennants
12) white; ice
13) a) Class Rules
14) #2 and #3 (both begin with "Raise")

PAGES 135-136
1) No
2) True
3) Four
4) Between the cake and cheese plate
5) No
6) Tapered
7) Scissors and a spool of ribbon
8) b) approximately 13
9) Pink
10) None
11) b) red plastic forks
12) Bananas (sliced)
13) Two
14) A purse

PAGES 137-138
1) False
2) The bottom edge of the field of blue
3) Five
4) Gold
5) Iowa
6) c) 1903
7) Three
8) First
9) Blue
10) G.A.R.; A
11) One
12) Two
13) Major (his name and rank are on the photo)
14) Five

PAGES 139-140
1) False
2) Yes
3) Yes
4) They are pointed
5) The first one
6) Four
7) c) black, orange, and cream
8) A drumstick
9) b) approximately 16
10) Red
11) The third boat
12) The second boat
13) a) high, high, low, low

PAGES 141-142
1) False
2) No
3) The flowers
4) No
5) No
6) Horizontally
7) Rolled-up sleeves
8) The fourth one; yellow
9) b) by the handle
10) White
11) Croissants, scones, muffins
12) The third
13) a) a red bowl resting inside a blue bowl

PAGES 143-144
1) It's a two-story building
2) Yes (in the back)
3) Yes
4) True
5) Yes
6) Blue
7) PT
8) Pink
9) Five
10) Turquoise
11) d) yellow, green, blue, gold, blue
12) Pink
13) The second and fifth buildings

PAGES 145-146

1) False
2) Left
3) A curtain
4) False (both are rectangular)
5) Two
6) a) a light switch
7) The bass
8) Three
9) a) J.W. (Jimmy Wakely)
10) b) 8 (including the one at the far left)
11) A horseshoe
12) Five

PAGES 147-148

1) True
2) Yes
3) No
4) False
5) No
6) Two on each side
7) Wood
8) Red
9) None
10) Brown
11) Three
12) b) 30 (six rows by five columns)
13) d) red paper, gold ribbon, no bow

PAGES 149-150

1) No
2) False
3) Red
4) Two
5) c) Uncle Sam
6) A ballot box
7) b) megaphone
8) Three (donkey, elephant, eagle)
9) They are all in the western half of the map
10) The U.S. flag; three times
11) The Capitol building
12) Zero

PAGES 151-152

1) Yes
2) True
3) *The Red Tent*
4) Horse
5) Clive Cussler
6) c) 9
7) *Gone Girl*
8) Spotlight
9) Four
10) *Half-Blood Blues*
11) *The Strain*
12) Six
13) b) circles
14) Flanagan

PAGES 153-154

1) False (one clock is like a cuckoo clock)
2) Cut off
3) Yes
4) 32
5) Do not enter
6) Yellow
7) Round
8) b) at the upper left
9) Three
10) Between 4 and 5; the 4 is represented as IIII.
11) White
12) c) B, D, A, C
13) Between the 2 and 4

PAGES 155-156

1) True
2) Celsius
3) The sun
4) No
5) b) 5 columns, 6 rows
6) Increasing heat (for water, drying, and ironing)
7) Black (or dark gray)
8) c) 7
9) The fifth column
10) a) Any solvent, Hand wash, Tumble dry
11) c) 32
12) Bleach
13) Three vertical bars

PAGES 157-158

1) True
2) Purple
3) 14
4) Green
5) a) elephant
6) They are in a plastic bag
7) Three
8) A red bird (Red from Angry Birds)
9) Pink
10) Large
11) Green
12) 5
13) a) approximately 5
14) Black and pink

PAGES 159-160

1) False
2) Baileys Crossroads
3) South
4) A star
5) d) McLean, Silver Spring, Landover Hills
6) 66, 295, 395
7) Red
8) a) N. Capitol St.
9) Arlington
10) b) 22 and 23
11) An airplane
12) b) black, full capital letters, italicized

PAGES 161-162

1) True
2) Horizontally
3) Snowmen (8 snowmen, 3 doves)
4) No
5) b) sleigh
6) Two (the others are green striped, multicolor striped, and red with sprinkles)
7) c) the left and right edges have semicircular projections not directly across from each other
8) Snowflakes
9) c) 11
10) It's half red and half green; in the upper-left corner
11) The lower-left quadrant
12) A plain cookie-colored angel
13) d) 95

PAGES 163-164

1) T.J. Maxx
2) Yes (Shell, in the fourth column)
3) Amazon; six spots (five with the "a" logo and one for Amazon Kindle)
4) A heart
5) c) Lane Bryant
6) Three
7) Mickey Mouse; Cinderella
8) New York
9) b) 12
10) d) neither is in the photo
11) Orange and white
12) They are separated from each other
13) Blue
14) Give the gift that sizzles

PAGES 165-166

1) The right half
2) No
3) Eight
4) Black and white (or brown and white)
5) c) 70
6) b) green and purple
7) Five
8) Black, blue, and green
9) a) on the far left and far right
10) Lower left (the large brown butterfly with light green stripes)

Image Credits

Alamy:
81: CalSportMedia

Deposit Photos:
109: Everett225

New York Public Library Digital Collections:
47: Billy Rose Theatre Division, The New York Public Library. "Barnum & Bailey greatest show on earth circus poster"

Shutterstock.com:
5: Stokkete; 9: Oleg Golovnev; 11: Botond Horvath; 13: Joseph Sohm; 15: Lukasz Stefanski; 17: Africa Studio; 19: MSSA; 21: Anton_Ivanov; 23: Neftali; 25: Zerbor; 27: Jiawangkun; 29: Rafal Olechowski; 31: Natalia_Maroz; 33: Monkik; 35: Revers; 37: Elena Schweitzer; 39: Peter Gudella; 41: Everett Collection; 43: Thinglass; 45: Mariakraynova; 49: Matyas Rehak; 51: James Steidl; 53: Kar Tr; 55: Everett Collection; 57: Andrey Armyagov; 59: Poznyakov; 63: Andrew F. Kazmierski; 65: Vladimir Salman; 67: Monkey Business Images; 69: Everett Collection; 71: Wallenrock; 73: Cobalt88; 75: DW Labs Incorporated; 77: Boykov; 79: Everett Collection; 83: Trekandshoot; 85: LunaseeStudios; 87: Popova Valeriya; 89: Poznyakov; 91: Nejron Photo; 93: Everett Collection; 95: Angelina Dimitrova; 97: Rawpixel.com; 99: Pavel L Photo and Video; 101: Icatnews; 103: B Brown; 105: Photo-Denver; 107: Oneinchpunch; 111: Bochkarev Photography; 113: Elena11; 117: Jose Gil; 119: Mariakraynova; 121: Filip Fuxa; 123: Marie Appert; 125: Everett Collection; 127: Yuganov Konstantin; 129: Ramunas Bruzas; 131: Lightwork; 133: Monkey Business Images; 135: Mariusz S. Jurgielewicz; 137: Joseph Sohm; 139: Shi Yali; 141: Monkey Business Images; 143: EQRoy; 145: Everett Collection; 147: Crossphoto; 149: Cienpies Design; 151: Niloo; 153: Warut Chinsai; 155: Shopplaywood; 157: Sean Pavone; 159: Aceshot1; 161: Elena Elisseeva; 163: Sorbis; 165: Aerogondo2

Wellcome Library, London:
7, 61

Wikimedia:
115: "The Knight's Dream," Antonio de Pereda; photo by Paul Hermans

Photo research by Amy Goldstein and Robert Leighton